DJINN & CHAI

PARDIS ALIAKBARKHANI

ISBN 978-1-990416-19-4

to extinguishing the past and lighting the future

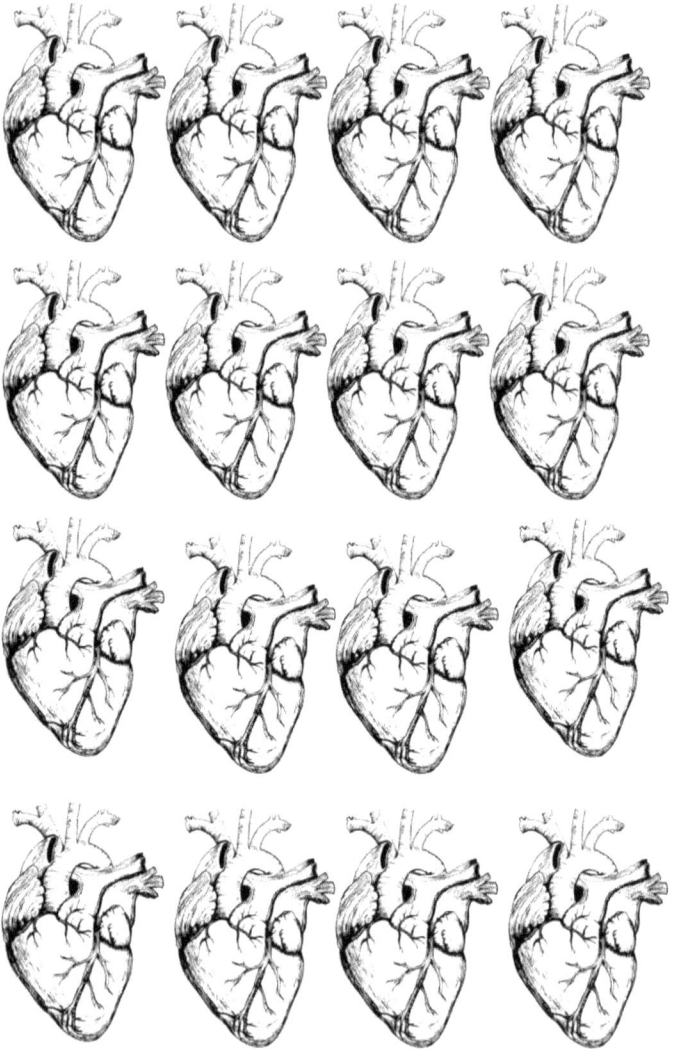

THE DJINN - (1)

i have severed memory of you from every major artery.
bled you out, femoral. expelled you in crimson clots that
bubble from my lips for years as i learn to forget the
taste of your name on my tongue.

you were intoxicating. a dizzying hallucination that
brought me in and out of consciousness, swirling from
one reality to another; yet in all of them, you are a blade.
and you cut me down before i have the courage to cut
you out.

i am too enraptured by all the ways that you make my
toes curl to realize how you also make my stomach
drop. the butterflies in my belly are dead moths
succumbed to your light.

for a time, i think you are the sun. it is years before i
clear my eyes and realize you are the mirage of a
flickering *'open'* sign in the desert. i built you up so high
i pinned you to the sky. desperate, searching, i mistook
the hiss and crackle of your neon flickering lights to be
the light that would illuminate me into love.

the light at the end of the tunnel that signals when a
journey begins, not dies. how desperate i was for that
light that i convinced myself that it lived in one person,
instead of existing all around us and in everything.

it has been many long years since i last heard your
voice. i hope never to hear it again. not for the
memories. or closure. there is no closure when violence
comes to sit at the same table as love. how could you
serve me cruelty and softness from the same hands?

and why did i take it? if i crept over eggshells for you,
why didn't she? or the others? how many women did it
take to feed your ego? why did it always take one more?
why did my pain satiate you the most?

it has been years. of writing. healing. loving.
discovering intimacy i hadn't known possible. learning
new ways to love and be loved. and for it all, i mostly
forget you. except for the days she lingers quietly at me
and i wonder if her pause will explode into anger. if her
smiling at her phone is a red flag the same shade as
another woman's lipstick. you are gone, but you are still
here.

a demon in human skin, shifting from blood and bone to
a chill up the spine, a trigger in words i never thought i'd
hear strung together again. how was i so convinced that
her love would fix what you broke? hope. i had hoped
her smile might disappear the memory of your rage.
sometimes, it does. not always.

the insecurities you left, craters on the moon. the
dimples on my thighs, scars on my cheeks. they remain.
the fear that reverberates through me and sends me into
fits of laughter and uncomfortable jokes when i just
want her to hold me through my tears. that remains. i
made you a ghost to my life and you're still haunting
me. djinn. everything that you want, with a price. fine
print. damnation.

she warms the water for my tea. keeps a cupboard
stocked with tea bags and sugar just for me. i bring the
mug to my lips and warmth radiates from my chest to
my stomach to my toes. she sweetens my drink with a
kiss on the cheek, a shared look.

but my mouth is full of salt. tears you pulled from my
eyes. a bitterness i can't speak in fear that she will
someday become you. why does no one talk about this?
how the living haunt us more than the dead?

when the love is great but the damage is greater. when
we find our way to our person before ourselves. the
surgery of dissecting our traumas from the love so that
we do not bleed the past into the future. how much we
cut. all that we lose in the unspoken.

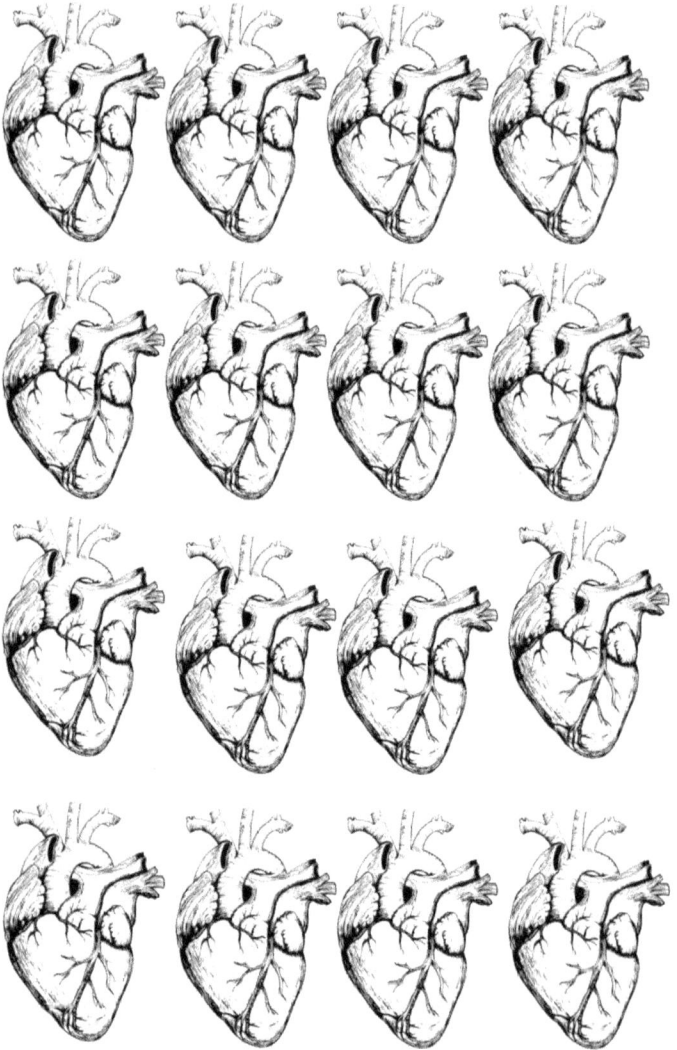

UNDEFEATED - (2)

it killed me loving you, a thousand times
it is deading to attach yourself
to a live grenade
i romanticized a gun because
only one bullet sat in the barrel
to confuse fear and excitement
so entangled by the two that i never divined
whether it was god or luck
that had me survive you

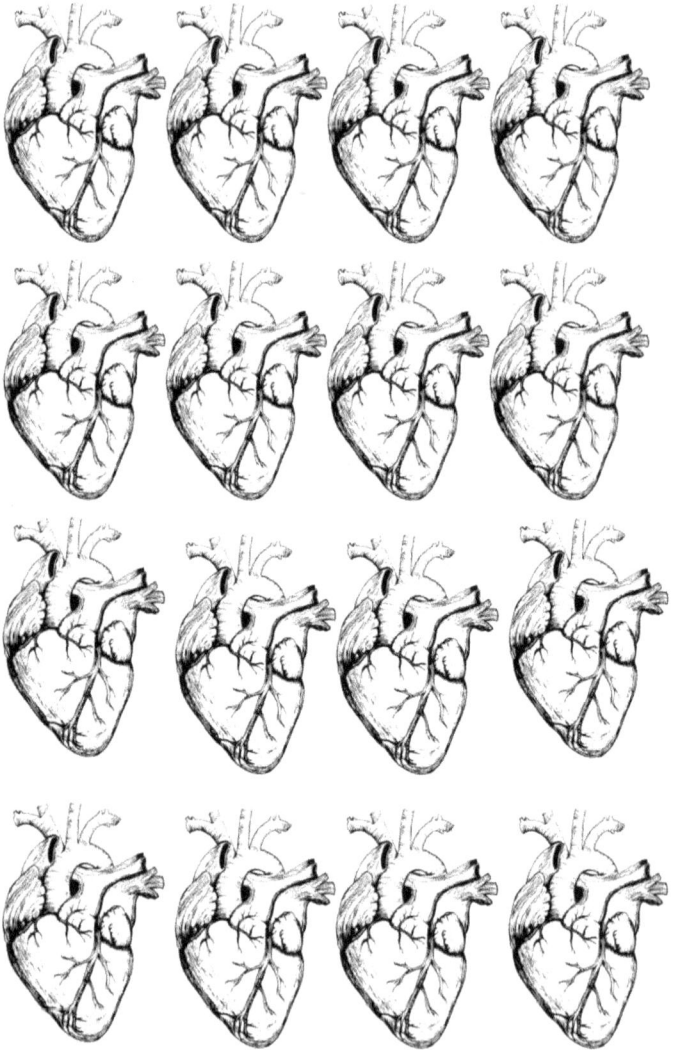

THE RESURRECTION - (3)

in between the blinks
the years that i scream into voids
that i call *mother*
i see his face in scars—self-deprecating jokes
my discomfort
when my wife touches me,
over an unsanctioned roll
or a spot of hair i missed
on my legs
in my morning shower

you're gone but you're here and i don't know how
to tell her

                          it's not her fault but you're still here
                                        you lit a fire inside me
                                                        and
                          you are the ash that blurs things between us
                          when she speaks and i hear you—she speaks
                                              and you *hiss*
                                        i try not to tell you what to do
                                              not that ghosts listen
                          but you have impregnated so much of my mind
                          that you could not afford the child support
                                                    you owe me.
                                              but neither can i.
                                        having peace of mind
                                                    is priceless
                                        and my frozen tongue
                                              thawed on her lips
                                        in kisses after hard conversations
                          where we are entirely made up of casualties
                                              the strategy of battle
                                              being *die for me*

and let that be enough—but it isn't enough
the fire encouraged me to cool my flames
especially as they strung me up
an autumn scarf
all summer fires that have long been extinguished
why are you still here?
i am happy now
in love
why does it still burn
why are you everywhere
why is she apologizing
for your mistakes?

why
faithful
carried by
the romance
of years
dedication
intimacy
becoming naked
in bed, in spirit
she has brought me home
from the loneliness you sprung upon me
her reward; the awakening that
we deserve more
than ghosts and fires can conjure
under a mountain of fallen soldiers
burning, fire
who am i?
to deny myself the lighter
after all the darkness
that has visited here
she deserves
all my light

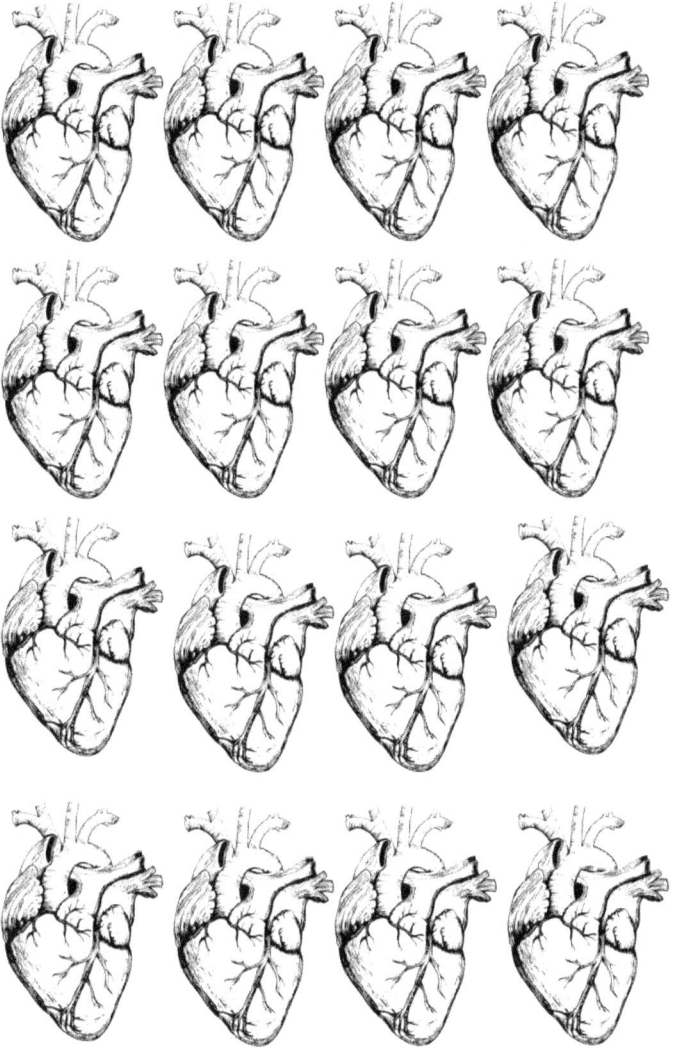

POISON IVY - (4)

calamine lotion
safe nightly routines
when i dream sweetly in my sleep
honey reverie:
skin to pillow, well-threaded sheets
a bug bite inflamed by a sun rash
a wind burn from rafting

the wild is tucked away again
put soundly in its bed
windows closed, doors locked
the night covering thick woods
with a starry blanket

the bites itch less
the burns are now soothed
the moonlight bathes us clean
from our discomfort
swaying us in a restorative cocoon

when the sun graces the horizon again
and we are made anew
we emerge with wings that spread further
to friends
who love us better than
our exes do

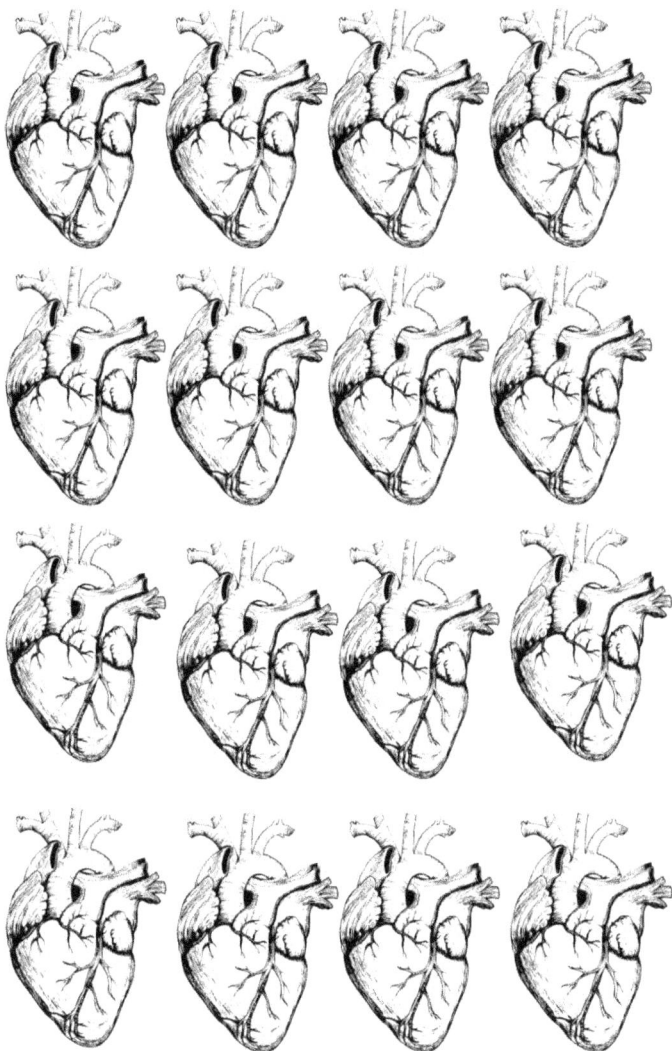

REMITTANCE - (5)

i glide into the new day
painting horizons with my eyes
choosing to forgive myself for staying so long
for the lingering hope that it was love
and not a black feather
i tried to paint gold

but
even the raven
is kind to their unkindness

i leave you in memories and burned pictures
frames that will never again be filled
in the silence that emptied my womb
from the desire to carry, birth
a son that could hurt me like you

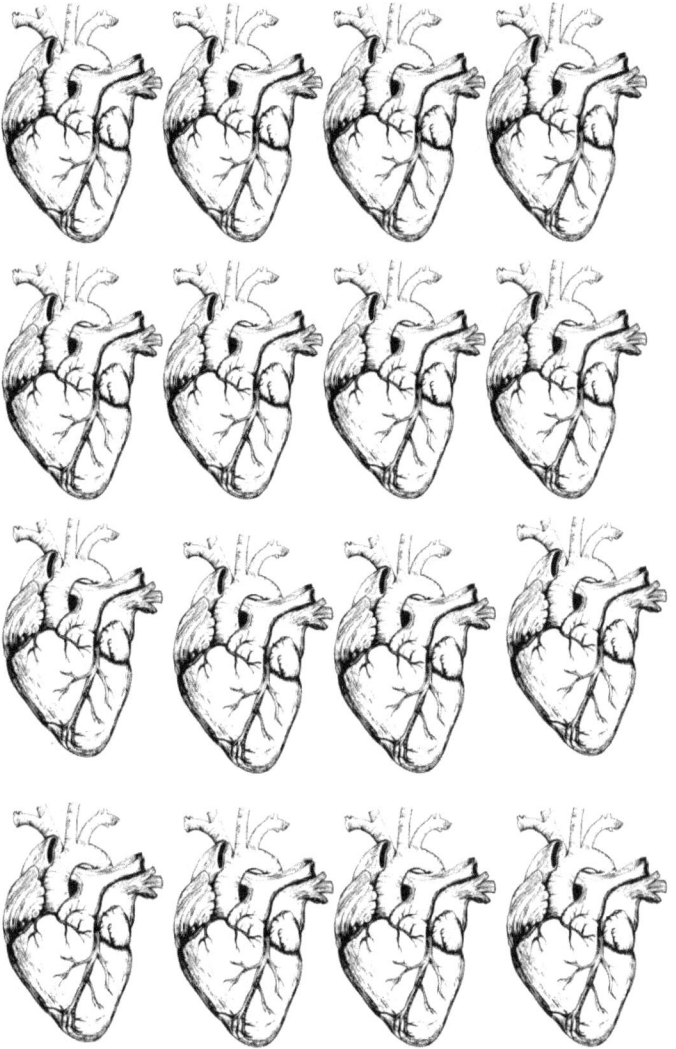

PERSISTENCE WITHOUT PRIDE - (6)

to love her is to vow
to not burden her with mistakes you made
and to love her
freely
not as an exercise in
who got it wrong
but a promise to try, with a full heart
to get it right

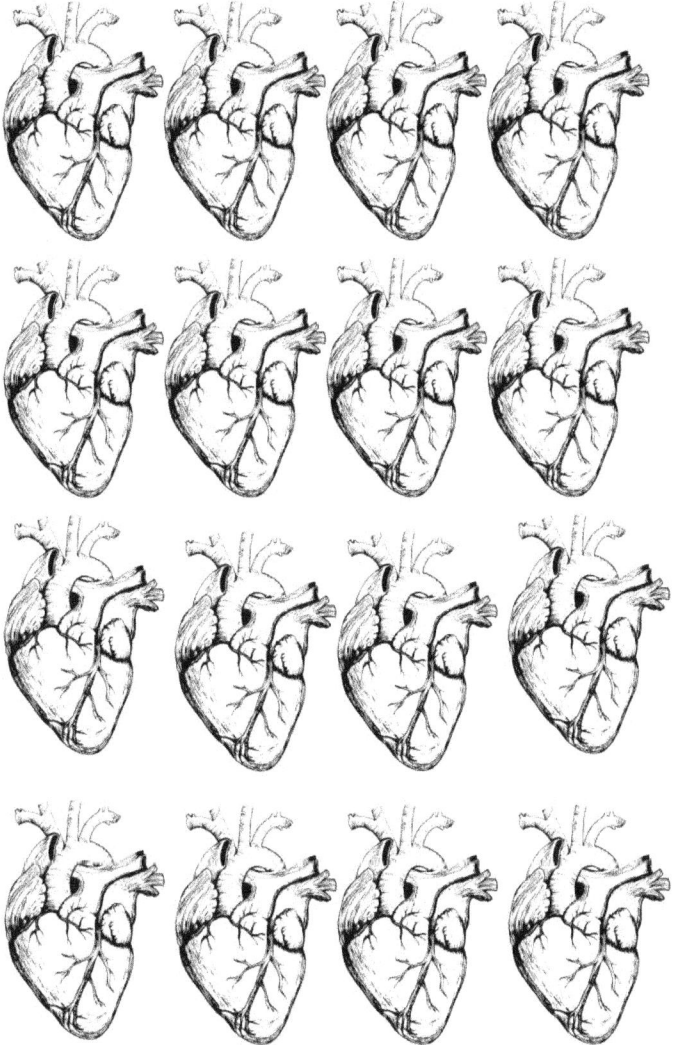

THE SKELETONS IN MY CLOSET ARE
MARIANETTES - (7)

endeavour to memorize the names
and favourite flowers
of every lover
so that when the relationship dies
you know what
to bury them with

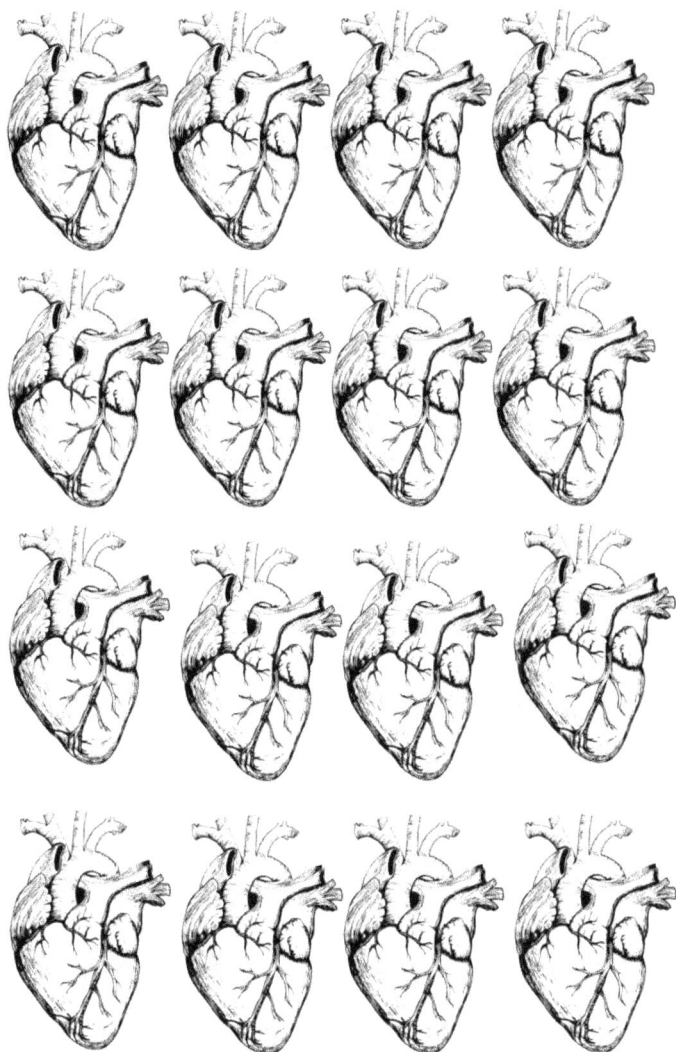

THE HOPE LIVES ON - (8)

fire water
who, in this solitude, will i find?
i don't want to walk around angry
with this axe in tow

they're all the same
i see his face everywhere
it pinches my nerves
to have waited on him
hand and foot—
and to have never earned
a good fingering back

i'm still adjusting to
the electricity of the emotional injury
after i would wrap my legs around someone
who sees me, bear-trap
as a zap to avoid loving

when my new lover says
they love my laugh
i remember when you said
i snorted like a pig—*looked like one, too*
compliments make my skin squeal
i set the whole barn on fire
and swallow the smoke fumes

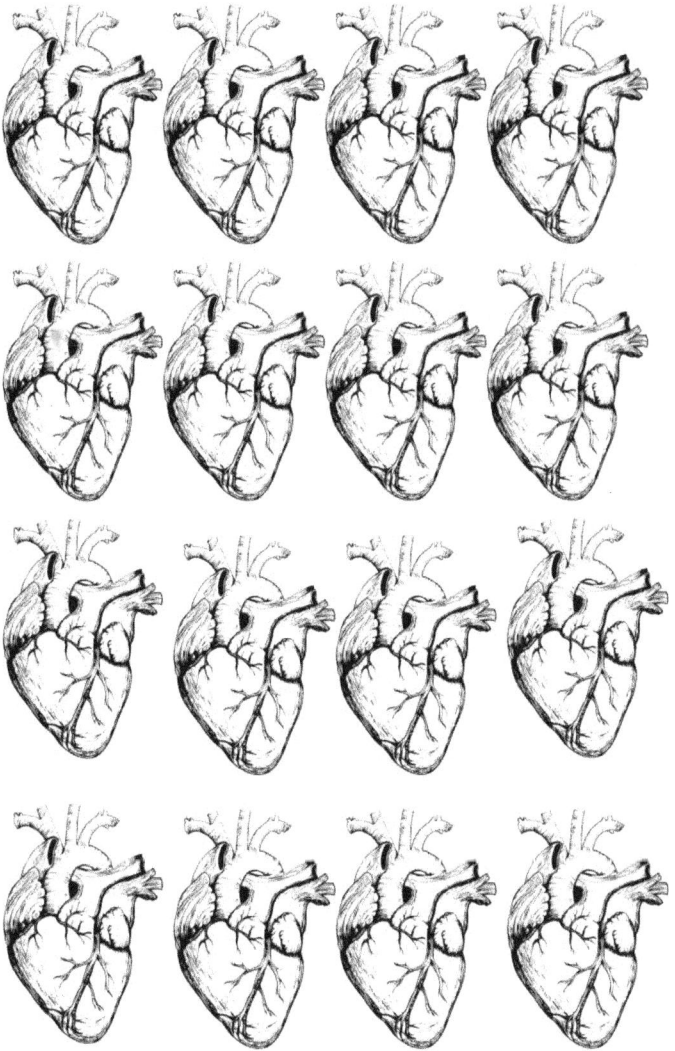

I SURVIVED YOU - (9)

you weren't a monster
though i swear i saw your skin shift
luminescent scales sparkle
in the night when you were prowling

you weren't a monster
just a hurt, fallible human
not so unlike me
a creature shaped by its environment
with sharp, white teeth

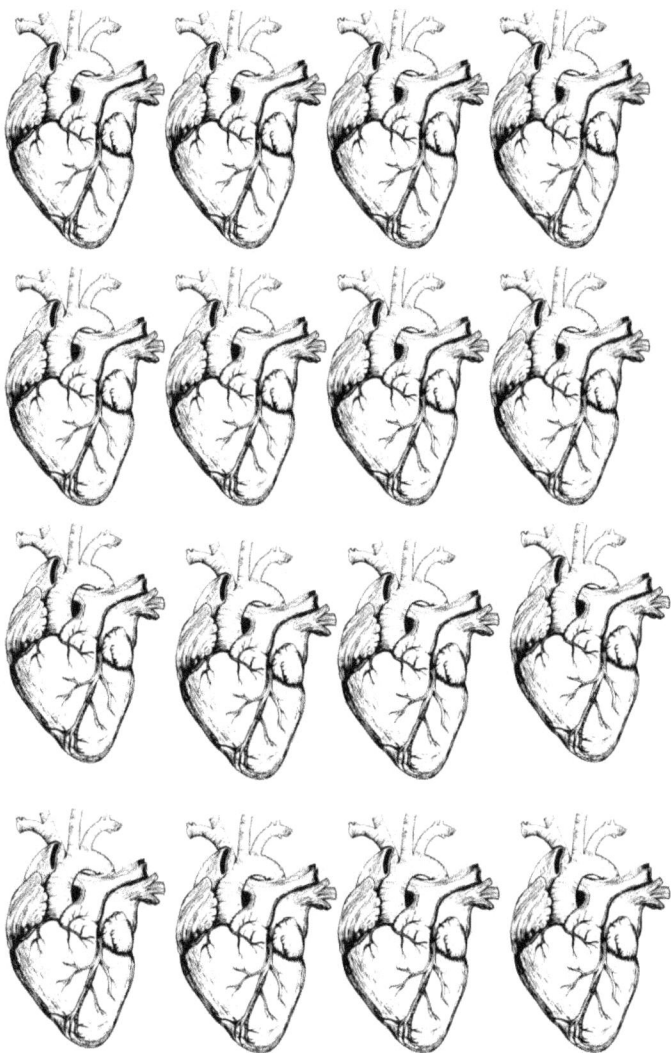

SUMMERS OF RED, HOT - (10)

we're on facetime together
and we're both
looking at me
mud in the water
moors painted green

i trip over my words with you
so often i instead
bite my tongue
teeth marks bruise the words
i can't say to you
because you're already not here

like *is it still abuse if you haven't cut me*
but you threaten to send me to
the devil's door?
if you love me, then leave me
the whiplash still makes me sore
is it still a danger if you cannot reach me
to choke me
so you feed on my tears?

i can't believe i survived you
when you sank me so low it felt like
putting me in the grave
when you poured soil over my mother's dreams
for me
when you fucked other girls
and called me a whore
i can't believe i spent money i didn't have
on you
like it could buy something
i would never own

your respect
to treat me with the dignity
of being a person and not a pawn

but my wife now, you should see her
she is my home away from home
she is the kindness, salt of the earth, loving
a beautiful, sweet girl
she has her mother's smile
and her father's smirk
and she looks prettiest on the open road
one hand on the wheel, one hand on my thigh
making jokes, telling stories
that fade with the summer sun

in quiet moments i exhale into her
and out from me
opening up pieces of her heart
she's kind and so funny

i carried so much shame before meeting her
and each day in this love makes the weight a bit less
until one day i will feel like air in her arms
i fly upon heaven under her caress

and i won't question how long it took to get here
only grateful that we did
and that
we can try again.

we can give birth to our little girl
and name her after the summer sun
i hope she inherits my wife's smile
and writes to us whenever she is gone

i hope our daughter has her mother's eyes
so she can see the good in people
that they don't see for themselves
and so that the world can know what god looked like
when i married her and made her belly swell

some people are robbers
because they break your heart, then steal it too
i couldn't love again for years after
he walked through.

when i started to heal myself, she appeared
by a bit of chance and a lot of luck
i met her open heart with nervousness
but fell years ago and still can't get up

i won't let anyone steal my humanity
or my ability to house love
i am four walls and a beating drum
i have no severed arteries
and i will love into love

heartbreak spun me on my axis
left me twirling into space
hurled me back as a slug on a rock
with a hollow celestial base

you are becoming history
and everything
you broke
is healing in ways i didn't think possible
every now and then
your pain
shoots back at me in disgust, nausea
a shame that lingers in my soul

i remind myself
that
even if she's mad at me, she loves me
even if she doesn't understand, she loves me
even if she's in love with someone else, she loves me
she has loved me into me loving me.

having someone who wants to embrace
every version of you
is medicine
god bless the omnipotent, the elements
especially water
that we are the soles that stand on
the greatest deliverer
spiritual bankruptcy
lets us believe we are not intentional beings
in this universe
that there is no grand design or code
to explain creation divinely
like when i think about the time we lost
as the time we needed
an expansion of the love we had for each other
into the love we build
because we learned to show up for ourselves

i want to be comfortable with you and
uncomfortable with you
i'd be happy broke with you
because i am with you
i would become a bonfire
to keep you warm
let me keep you warm

i kiss the worry out of her mouth
never letting her spend a night

wondering if my eyes still dart over to her
sure enough; i'd never doubt it
i can't wait to kiss her stretch marks
her soft skin
her delicate hands
she is the only music i hear

i'm not afraid to forget you
i held on for so long because i couldn't
afford to lose the love, too
but now i
crave the poetry of this new journey
her and i are on

i know sometimes
you're in the room
when she's quiet and it makes me sad
and tears prick at my eyes
because you said i was annoying
and unloveable
and i believed it

your hatred is diminished by her love
it's quieter without you in my ear
you weren't *in* the room before—
you *were the room*
and every moment with her
you disappear more into vanishing
evaporating into thin air

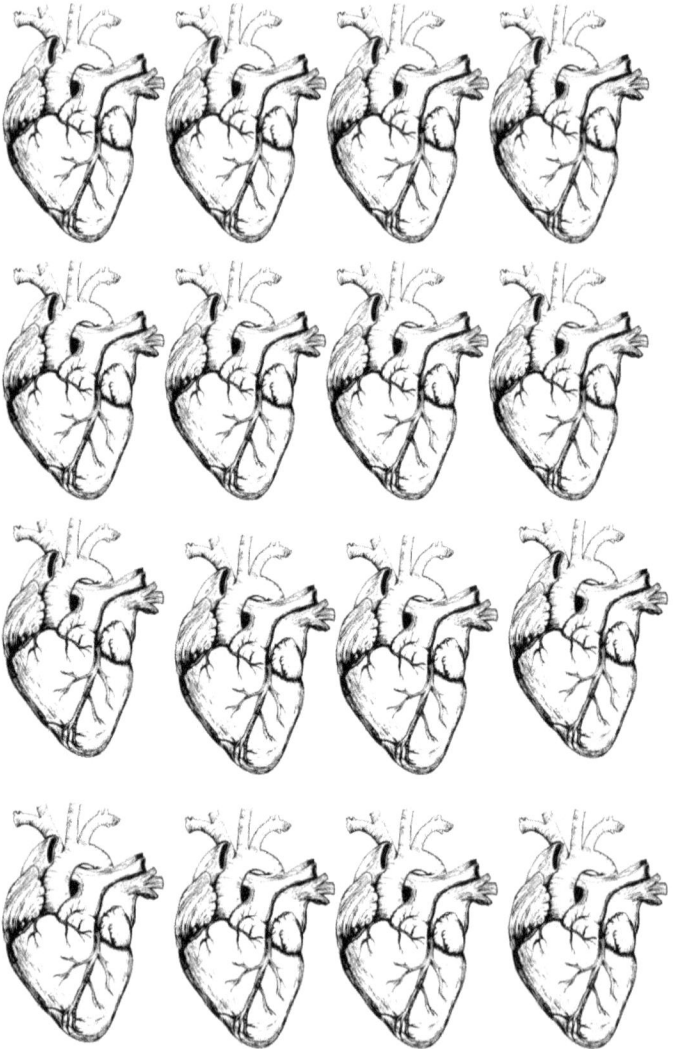

YOU'RE NOT EMPTY INSIDE, YOU'VE JUST
FORGOTTEN WHO YOU ARE - (11)

i've become
so blinded by my ego
sometimes
i forget my humanness
is no different than yours
and that you have a right to history
with a spirit that isn't mine
a connection that differs from ours
a bit of longing, questions
what ifs
that is a space for you
and your heart
and questions and hope and heartbreak
i can't touch
a street i can wander without destination
because there is no final destination
when it comes to where your insecurities
will take you
to love you is to trust that the love we have
and the life we choose to build together
is where you want to come home
and that won't need a roadmap
or convincing
it will feel as natural as breathing
and if i ever make you short of breath
or loving me feels more like a prison sentence
than a homecoming
give us both the freedom
to be marveled at again
the way i love you now
with my heart in your hands
far out of my chest

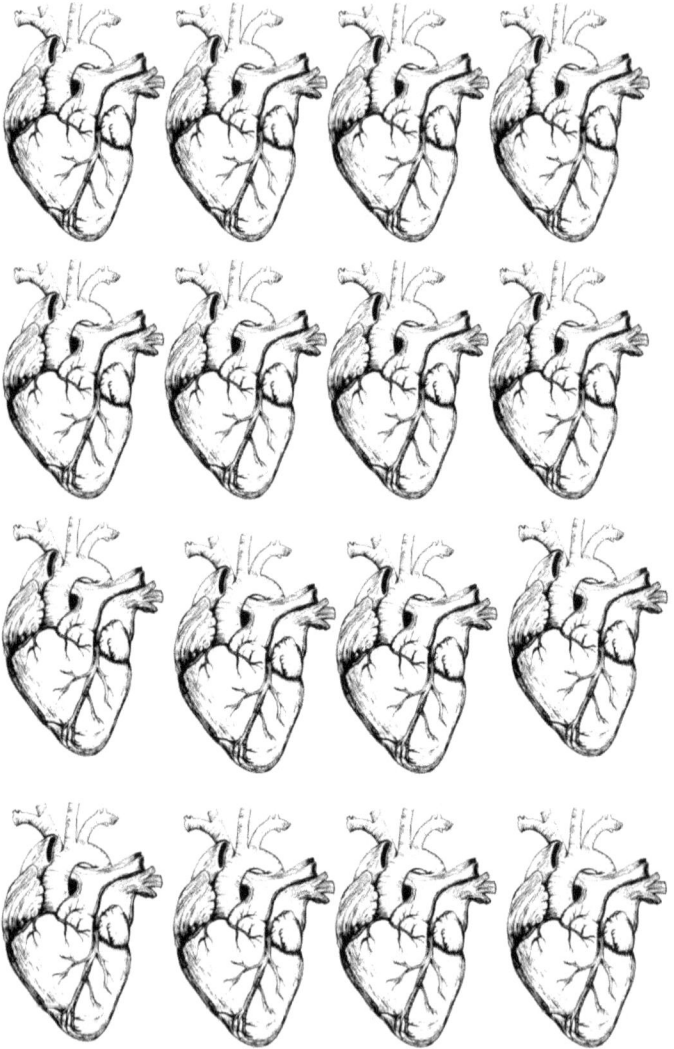

YOU CRAWL BEFORE YOU WALK - (12)

red oceans and green skies
i circle and wane
on a barge
drifting far, far away
at the core of all the faces
i wear
there is a real me
a touch of humour
lust
and loving.
the real me is creative
mother
fighter
healer
lover of all creatures
a believer in the energy
that some call god
and others call nature
and in either story
the root is creation.
this universe is entirely perception
we are real as we feel we are
kept floating away from realities
where there is a real version of us.
something concrete, immutable by time
or grief
all the terrible things that happen to us
that bleed us into a new person, a crime.
i still don't know who i am
outside of my pain
and i stopped looking because
i am terrified to know if there is nothing that remains.
if i'm entirely made up of people who broke my heart

and the ways it shattered
in my chest for years
before anyone noticed that i was
dying inside.
what if the shell is all of who i am?
there is no depth, no core, no center
where i bloom from, a door marked *do not enter.*
all that my face says is what is
i was never going to be a writer
or a healer or a poet
without my trauma i was destined
to be a room temperature tea
not unforgiveable but unremarkable
favoured by few.
if i am only a matter of
who and what broke me
then i am grateful that
some of my greatest heartbreaks
were the people i love.
drawing their boundaries in chalk
while i ran out of masks to choose from
to justify my selfishness
and the way i twisted my reality
to understand friendship as a right
and not a privilege. all love is from god.

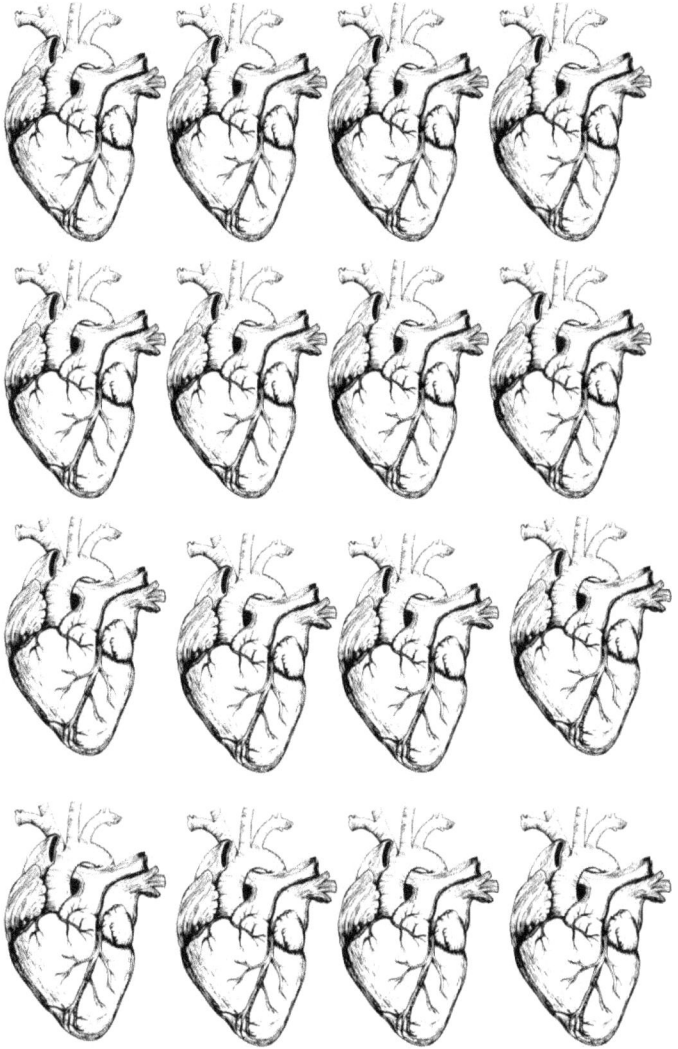

I COULD BE YOUR FAVOURITE - (13)

you convinced me
that i needed to be loved
with the lights off
and i believed you
and the weight of that
forced all the lights on
in my house

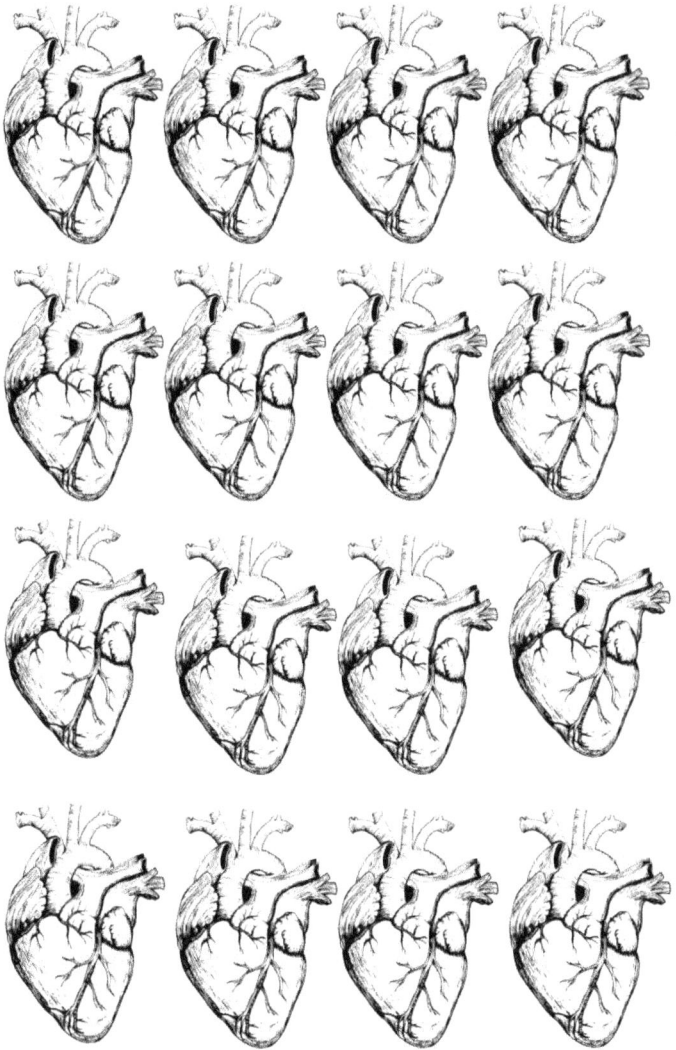

THE PUREST TRUTH THERE IS - (14)

i am the only one
who can save me
from losing myself
to the spiral of my thoughts
from sinking so low
into the woman
you made me believe i am
instead of the fire
i was born from

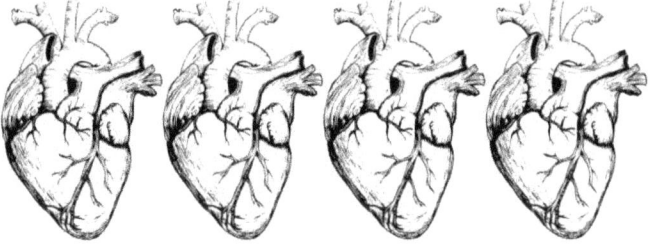

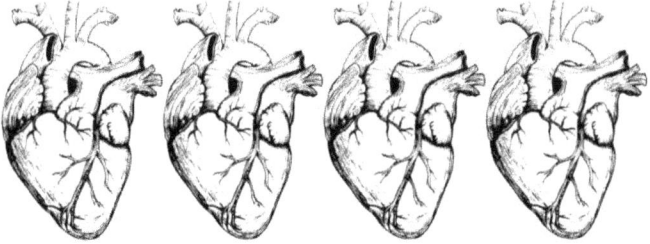

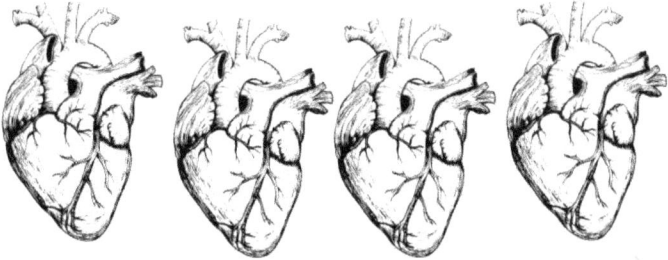

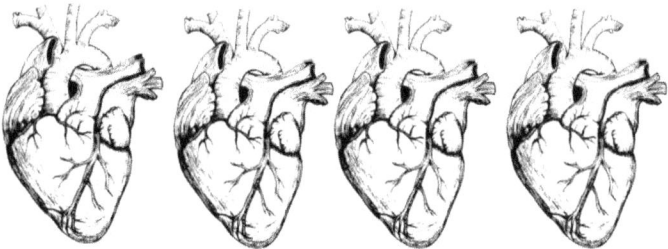

A TOTAL PACKAGE - (15)

accepting that
my pain
projected
into the kind of hurt
i invited into my life
and called love
is a different kind of agony
because it means admitting
that i am part of the cycle
i've been trying to escape

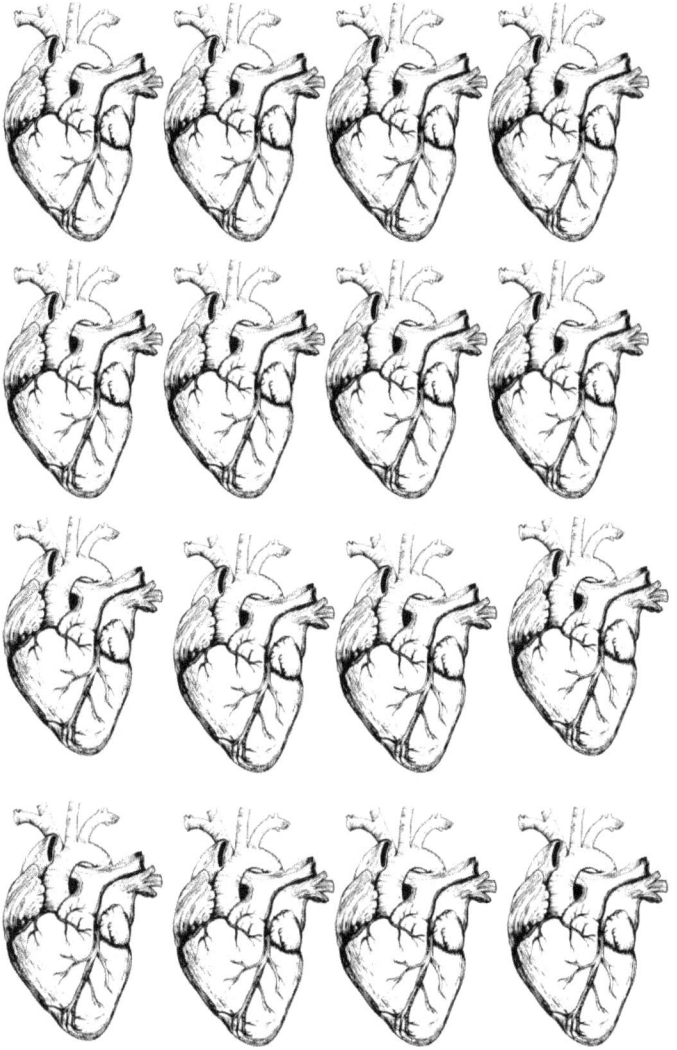

LIGHTS AND SIRENS, BABY - (16)

and i have become
a pillar of salt
for looking back
at what is done
the oceans that have dried up
if i am being delivered
from you
i won't look back
i have had my fill to drink
the salt i won't carry

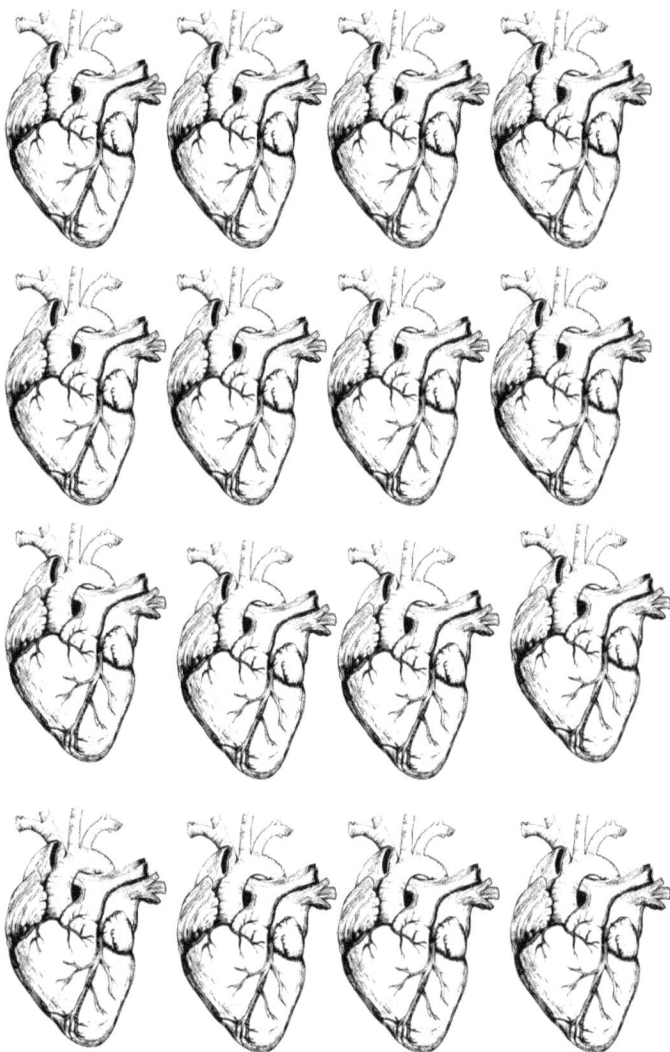

DIG HER UP, I WANT TO SEE HER FACE ONE
LAST TIME - (17)

you are the face i imagine
when i ponder missed opportunities

but you were a ghost
even when you were standing next to me.
always disappearing into another frenzy
walking through me
floating towards something else—
what i wouldn't have done
to know what it took
to exorcise our house
and make it
a home.

you made me a young widow by
deading everything i thought i cared about
while i searched for parts of you i could cling to
haunting myself with questions
you can't answer
because you were never really here.

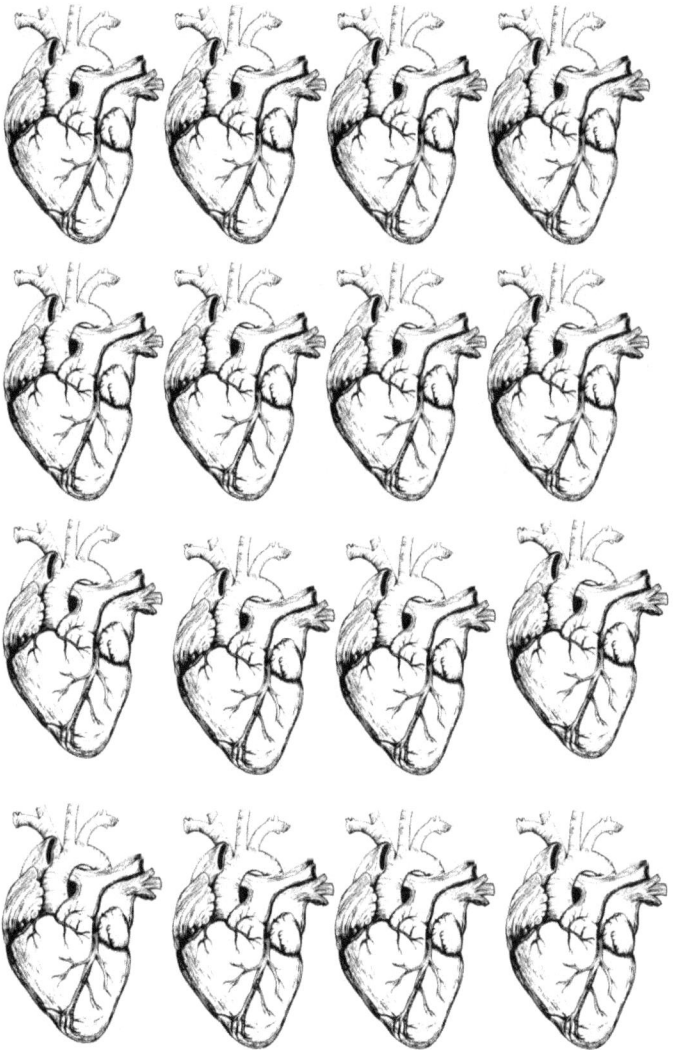

PUSHING BACK THE DAY - (18)

i am
pawing through the morning paper
scraping the barrel of my junk mail
and social media pages i should have
long retired
when my cat purrs and taps my paper
and my dog nudges my phone
with her nose
before she cradles her head
in my lap
i have unanswered messages
that can wait another hour
when a heart on four legs
calls to me, yearning for connection
i push back the day
another hour
and i answer
love's call

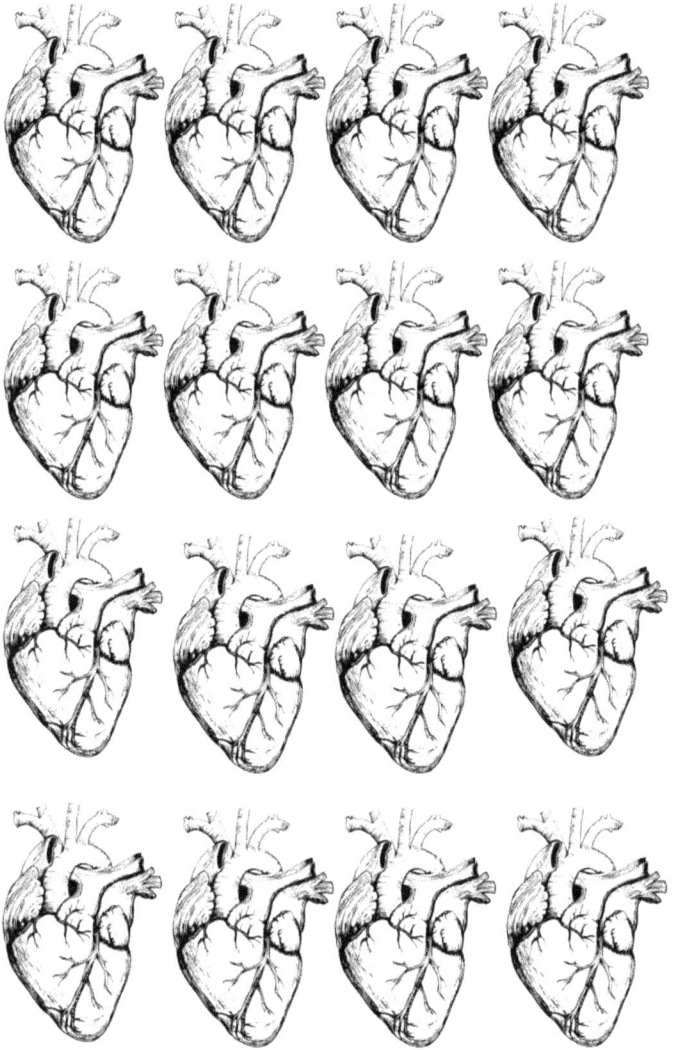

STOP, LINE ONE - (19)

what i allow for myself
is the message i send my daughter
when i let a lover walk in and out of me
like an open door
i tell her
access to you is not a gift
when i bite my tongue and leave impressions
on the organ
that was once a spring board
for words to dive off of
i am saying
your silence is more loveable than your voice
and i know the statistics
how it takes
7 attempts for a woman to leave
before it sticks
or she dies
because society told her
access to you is not a gift
and
your silence is more loveable than your voice
and i will be damned
if my mother survived
only for my daughter to inherit
her heartbreak

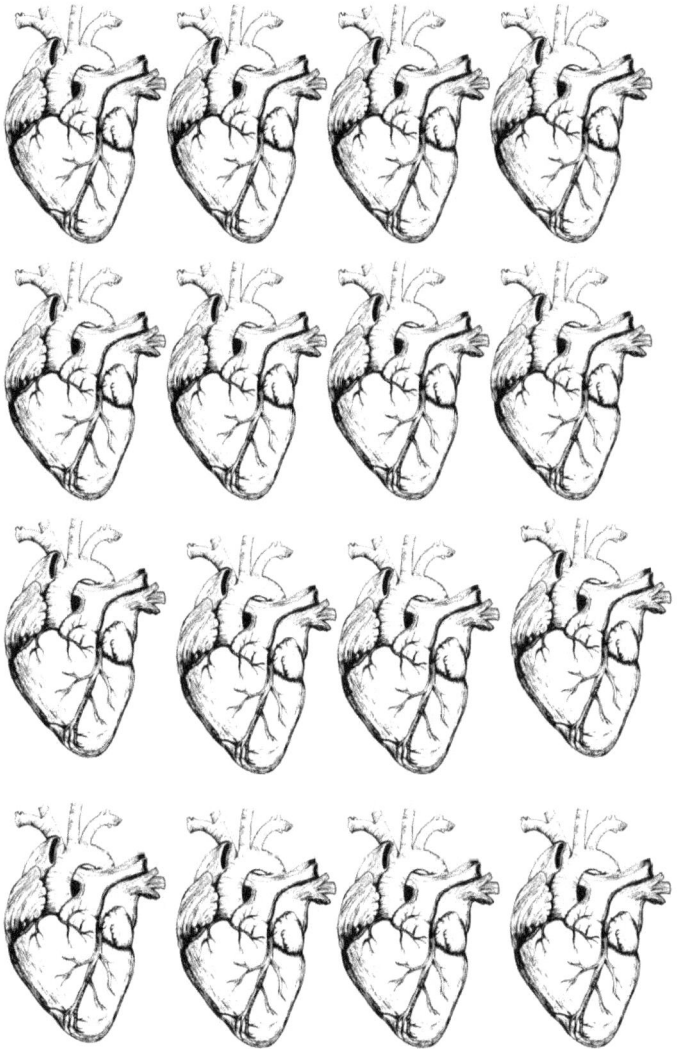

KISSING THE WOUNDS - (20)

"well no one died, what's the big deal?"
yet

does your son
your nephew
your friend
your brother
your cousin
your coworker
have to kill me
before
you agree
he is a threat?
how much violence
is acceptable
for a man to
beat into a woman's consciousness
before
it becomes
a big deal?

he pushes her
a little harder this time
chokes her
for a little too long
and
then
you say

"how could he do something like this?"
and the ligature marks form a signature
that says
how could he not?

WHAT IFS ARE A SNARE - (21)

i deliver myself from
the feral instinct to give in to the wild world of
temptation
you
us—we
could have been different if i were
more patient, understanding
and we could forge a nest of our own
hibernate through the winter
with your mother wounds
and my daddy issues
and forget about the bared teeth
the carnage
the other women.

we could never retire to instinct
of reaching for each other, paw to paw
clawing at the idea of forever
and maybe we wouldn't have to
by giving into the temptation of *what ifs*
and the perils of the untamed *what is.*

the truth is in the woods
among the trees
witnessed by god, the birds, sky, moon
you are the bear
and i am the meal
i cannot be consumed by the idea you anymore
because giving in to you
will always mean
cutting me down to the bone

and i can't keep sacrificing myself
to an animal

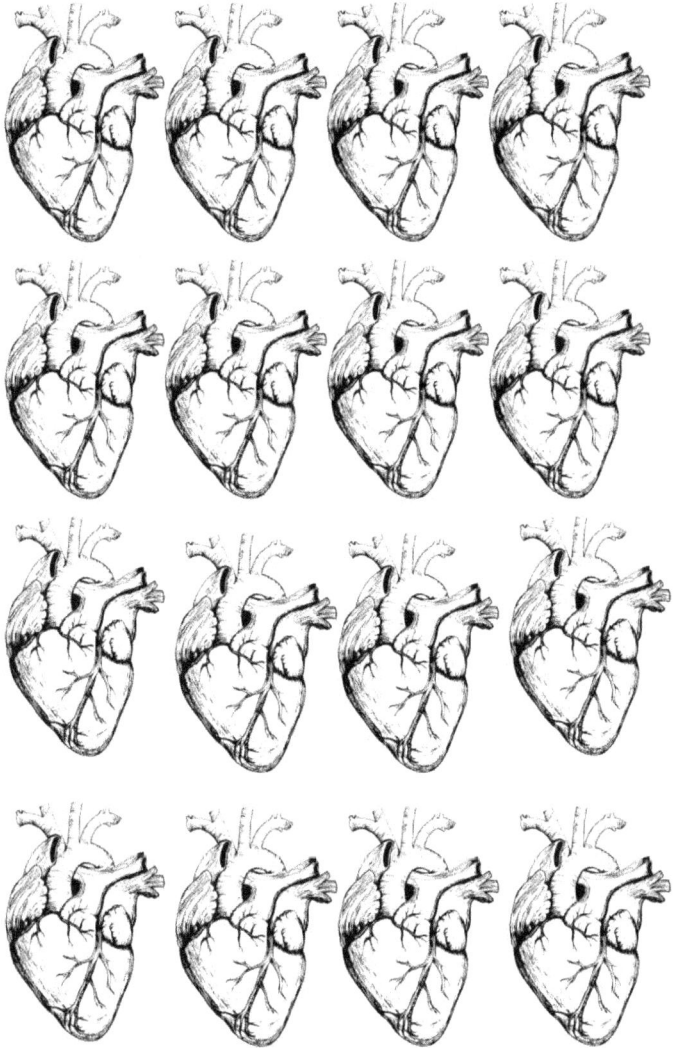

THE CAT RETURNS - (22)

entertaining flames of the past
as if they can still warm me
is cold to my new loving
and the person i have invented
in the summers that i had no one to love
but myself

when i was a young woman
new to the ways of love
i imagined everything was a consequence
of divine intervention

cupid's bow
that things would just click
as if i'd been struck
with an arrow
that could tell me the difference
between love
and being struck
with a stick

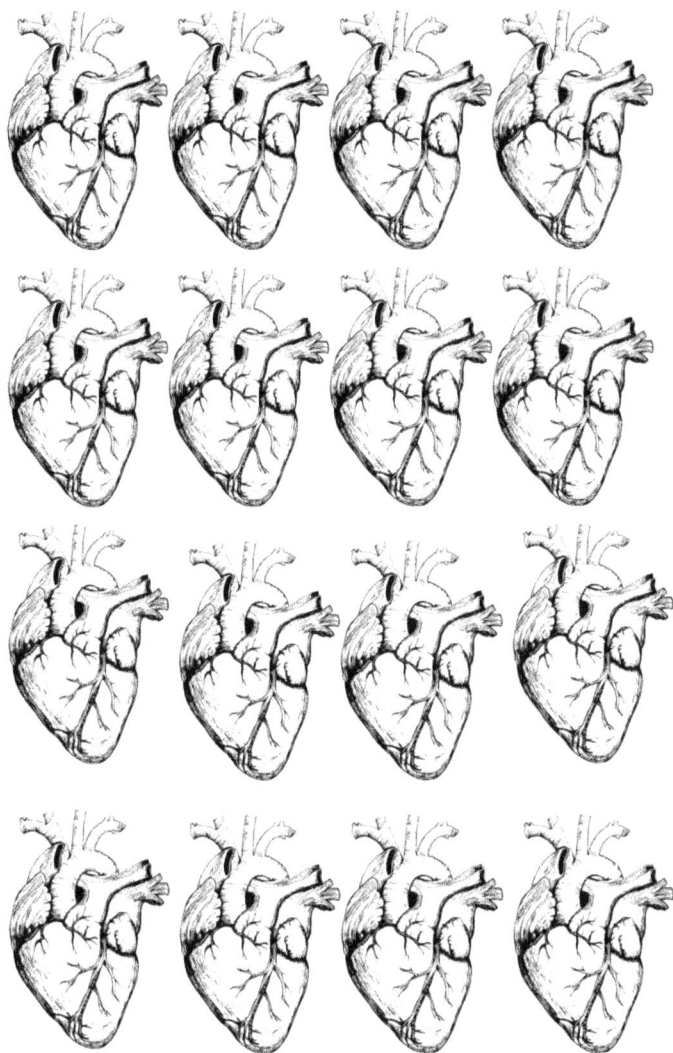

TMS - (23)

i would have died for him i cry to my mother

yes she coos

and he would have killed you

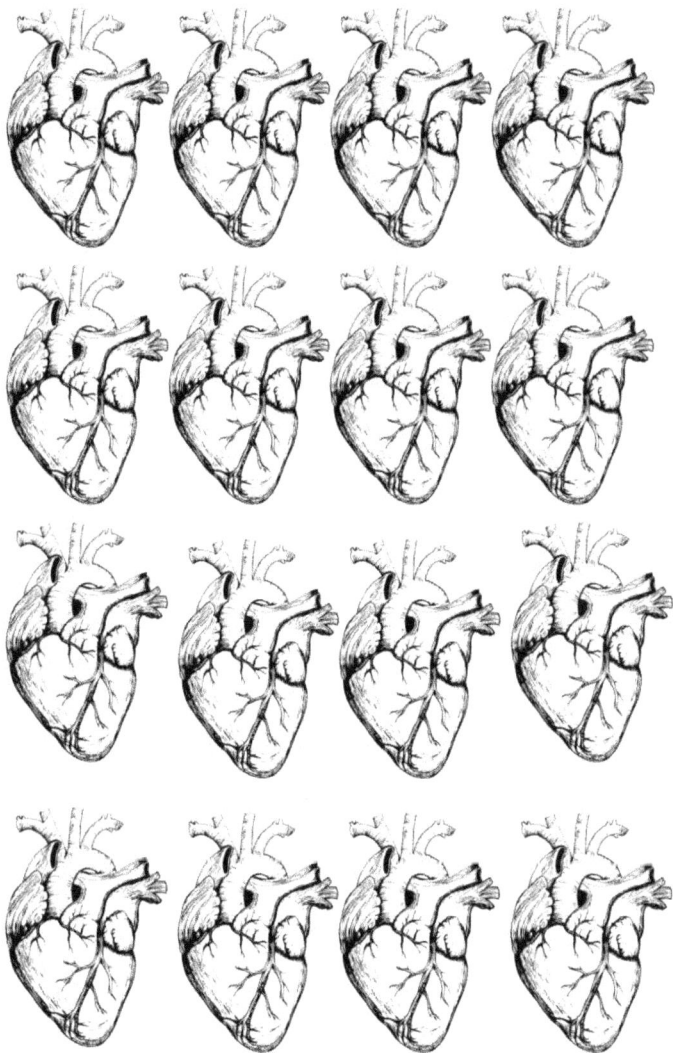

DEAD TIRED OF DEAD RINGING - (24)

do not lend the cruel voice in your head—
the one that echoes the taunts of schoolchildren.
your ex-boyfriend.
your ex-girlfriend.
your critical mother
your absentee father.
an ear.
do not lend it your thoughts
for it will surely overrun them.
you are worthy of kindness
and you must speak it to yourself first.

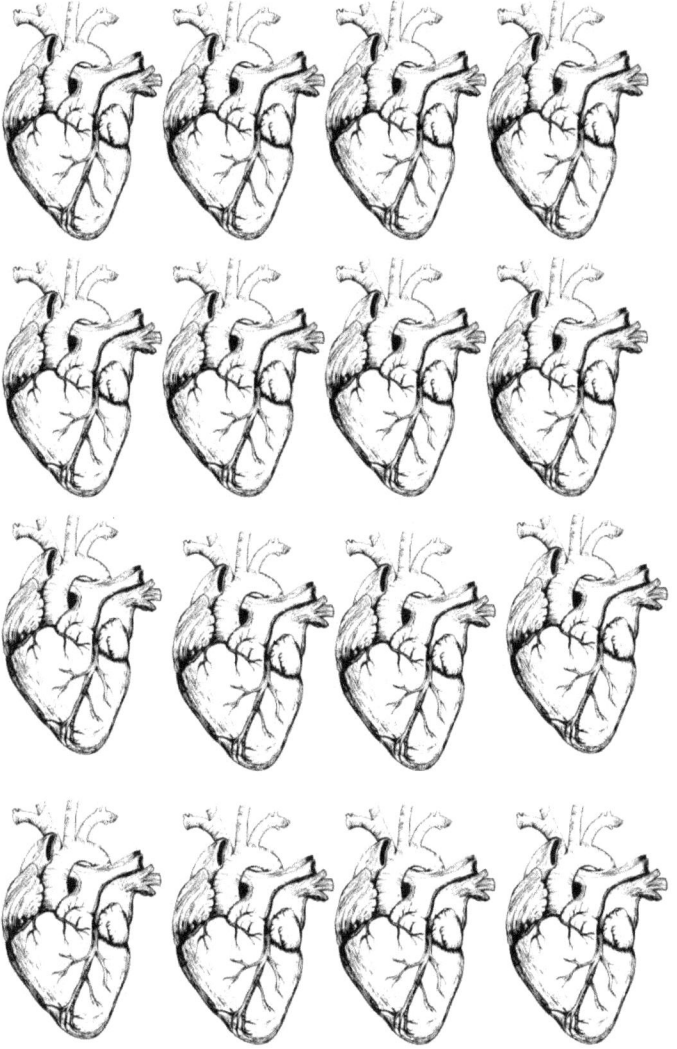

IT BECOMES YOU - (25)

i have seen raindrops
fall on my wrists.
and become voicemails to my ex.
my father and my mother
look at each other once every few years
like the divorce is not final yet
and they still have a chance
to be unbroken.
and all the while i so desperately
want to be the kind of person
who does not repeat my mistakes
but find myself
always in the process
of loving people
and breaking my own heart
while standing in the rain.

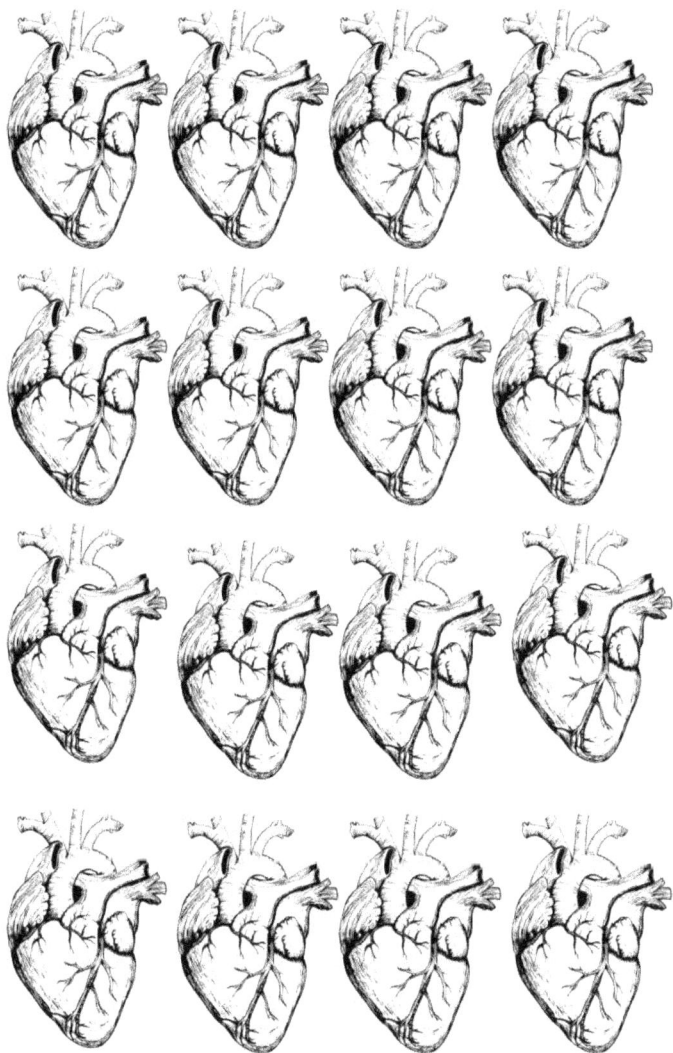

THE SALVE THAT SAVES US - (26)

i adopted two cats
a calico and a tortoiseshell sister pair
that were found in the rubble of the city
with curdled milk in their hair.

one stomps when she walks and falls over
on a whim; impulsive, clumsy, playful
if we were sisters, we'd be twins.

one is light on her feet and floats into my bed
she's stoic, graceful, cunning to the house mice
whose heads she collects.

when the world is dark, i see the light in their eyes
when it is heavy, i feel their feet hop weightlessly
across my chest.
they fight and tussle, smashing mugs
that'd been sitting prey on my desk
shattering my focus
splitting it away from my unhappiness.

the calico's favourite toy is a fabric banana.
the tortoiseshell's favourite toy is the calico.
when they sleep beside me, the three of us
all snore the same snore.

i forget my heartbreak for a moment
when i toss a crumbled receipt for them to fetch
or fill their tray with more than a handful of treats
they dust my clothes with their fur

which i notice
when i, wearing all black

am already at the office
and realize i am always
carrying their love with me.

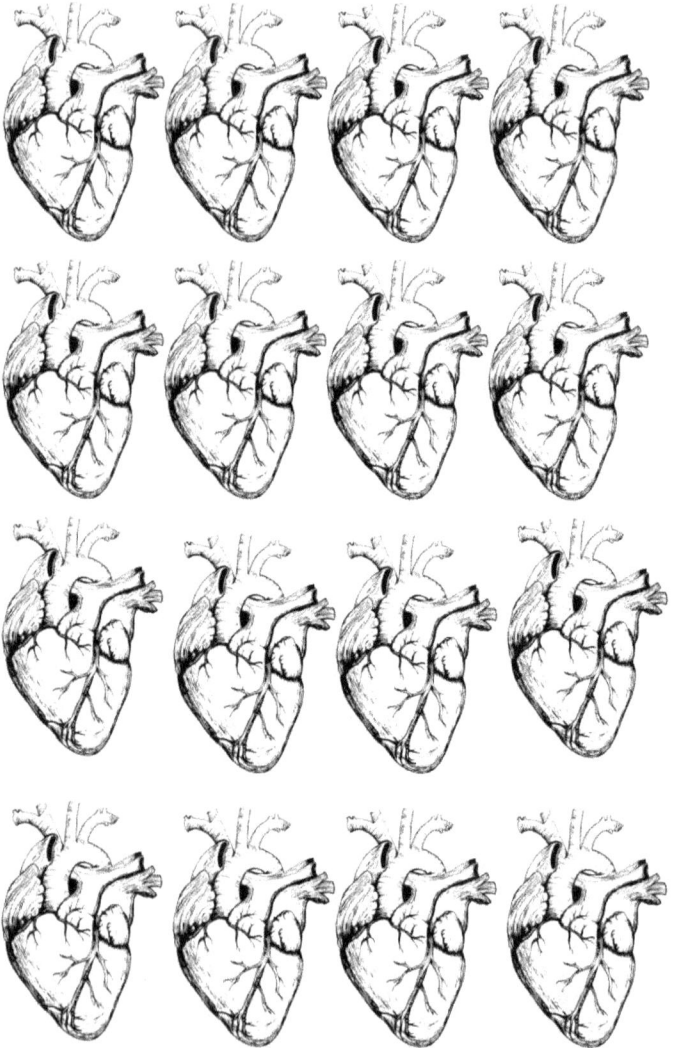

THE PEDASTAL DOESN'T SERVE US - (27)

to my father:
i am sorry that i blamed you
for things you did not break
to my father:
i am sorry for the things you did break
and how long it took me to forgive them
to my father:
i am sorry that i distanced my humanness
from yours
as if raising two daughters
would give you all the answers
and not more questions
but that first heartbreak
you walking out the door and not turning back
for years
never coming back
in the way that mattered
because you always had one foot in, one out
that has shaped the way
i have reached for every door with love behind it
my entire life

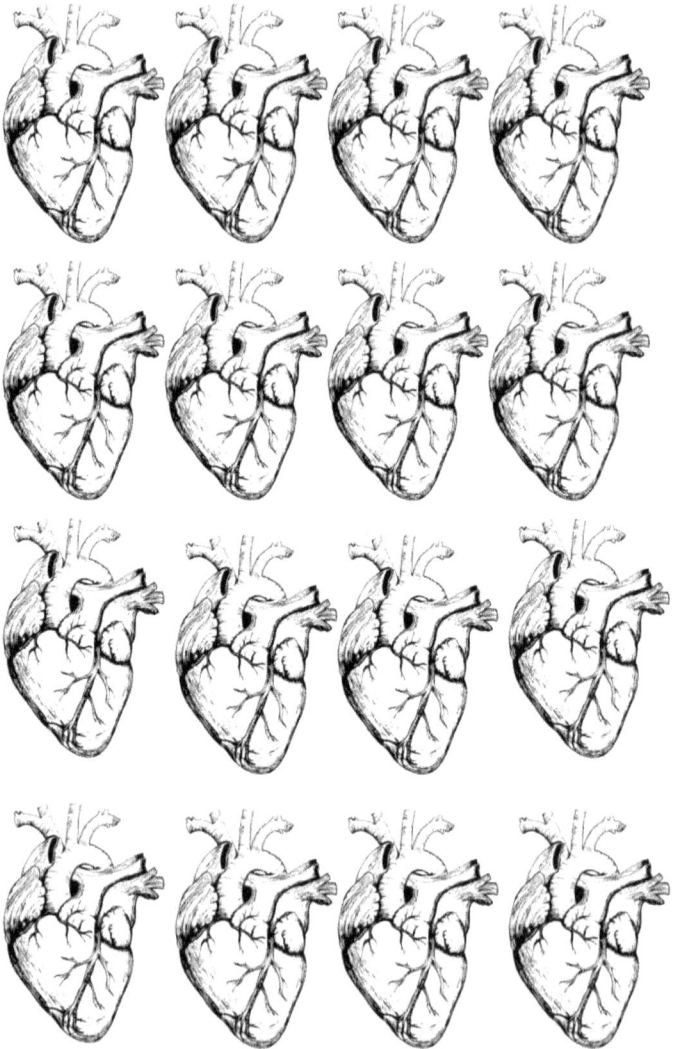

I HAVEN'T SEEN THE END YET - (28)

the red flags i've waived proudly
not seeing their hue—left whispers of opportunities
lovers that could've been true.
i wanted to be better so i became better.
i didn't want to be a crimson moon.
not if it meant suffering to my own heart
those i loved, too.
i am still unlearning all the red.
that my partner is a person outside of me.
that she was raised in a different town, with different
parents, with doors never barren wreathes.
she won't always understand my pain.
where i am coming from she has not been.
but we are magic in the way that we make promises
to always close the distance and in understanding,
meet.

                    the air washes out of my chest
         when her replies deviate from the script i've written
                         perfectly in my head. when she offers logic
              in substitute for the comforts i sometimes crave.
a maroon sky tells me our disagreements mean the love
                                   is not here to stay.
                  like the slammed doors of my childhood
         and my father packing up his car on a rainy day.
         the colours change and we hold each other close
                  she accepts my red, my orange, my yellow.
     she keeps me green because she inspires me to grow.
                  in the blue i find the calm of letting go.
     we celebrate the purple of our love together in lilac
                              bundles i plan to gift her.
pink lipstick smears on my wrist when i blot the shade
                                   to sheer.

i met her in red and again in the rainbows.
all that we are is the acceptance of what we've been
and all the journeys that still
have yet to paint us.

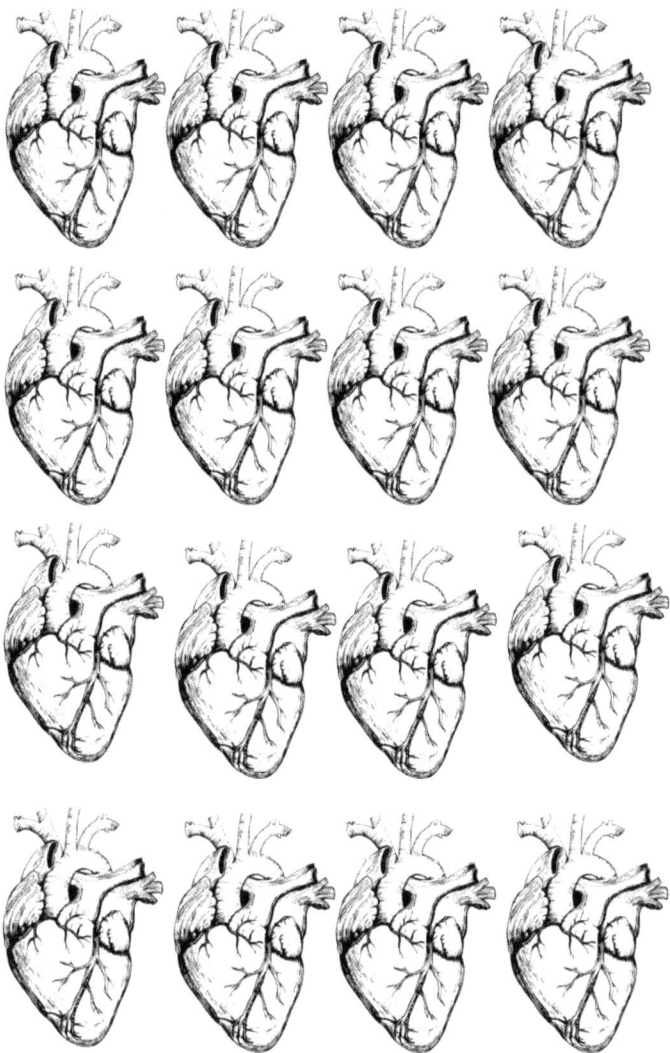

THE CONSOLATION PRIZE IS WORTH HOW
MUCH? - (29)

you deserve more than to be a
                              reminder of where he can
                                        stick his pride
                              and leave his mercy behind.
                                 grief is the last act of love.
                         the last one you need to experience.
your mind knows that.
your heart will, too.
what doesn't bend, breaks
and what breaks can be restored.
if only
you stop giving away
the pieces.

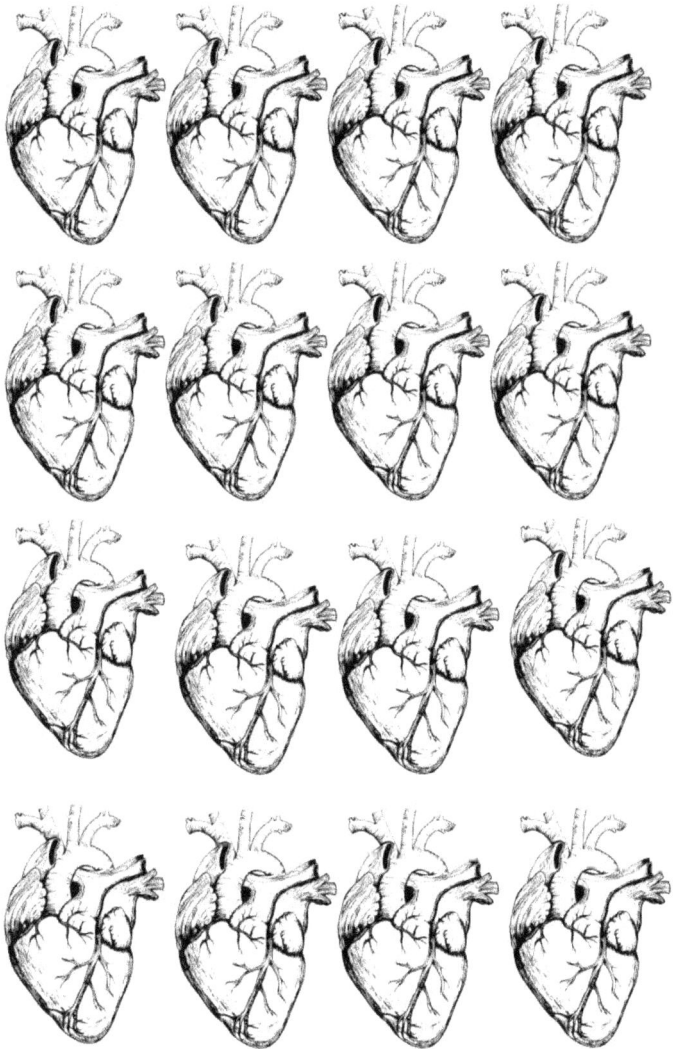

FORGIVENESS ABOVE ALL - (30)

i choose to forgive my parents. not just because of the fact that as i've grown older, i have realized that my father is just a guy. my mother is just a girl. no wiser or more cruel than any other. flawed, to be certain, but no more than the average flawed and loveable human.

i forgive them and the poor choices they have made masquerading as loving ones. the formative years where their trauma bled into mine. the inheritances i didn't ask for.

it's a choice i made when i chose to live my life in the service of love. after the realization that forgiveness is the ultimate act of love. paired with the knowledge that someday i will weep over their gravestones and there will be no one left to be angry at but myself.

so i mourn now. i mourn the childhood i didn't have. the softness and understanding and yes, the weirdness i craved that was never fully met.
i mourn the family dynamic that we couldn't have because survival meant less room for joy. i mourn that so i can celebrate what we did have; resilience, humour.

i mourn now so i can use the time we have left not heartbroken, but full from the knowledge that i can take the lessons of love without the cycles of abuse that almost destroyed them.

i forgive because anger is not the part of love i want to carry when they are gone. i don't want to bring it home to my wife and kids. it will not become me.

the breaking ends now.

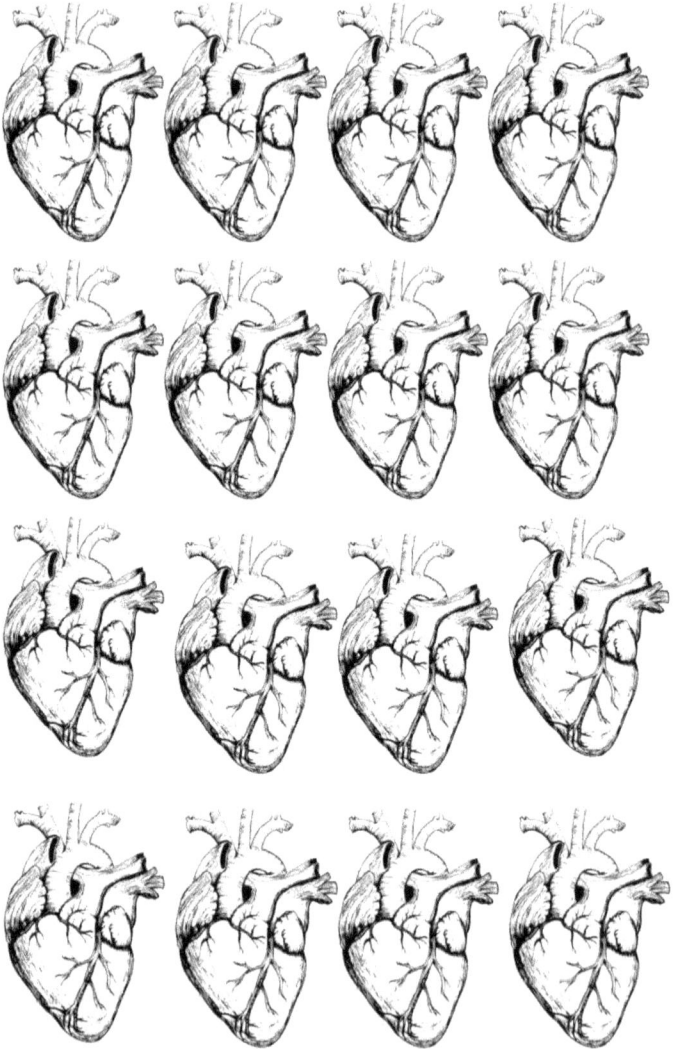

OH WELL, OH WELL - (31)

all that was here before
will be here after
so i wonder:
i wonder if she had space in the closet too
or if her things only lived in the nightstand
first drawer of two
if her slippers shuffled where i stumble
to the bathroom at 6am
half-asleep and frozen
from us and the dogs
sharing a crumpled sheet on the bed

did she suspect in her dreams
that 'i love you' was a holding place
for someone else to wander in
and take the first and second drawer
where her love lived?
i wonder if i'll know the signs
when our time comes to an end
when the love becomes more tiring, tedious
than new and exciting.
how will i know you've fallen out or love with me
will it start in sighs and end with looks
of glaring resentment?
will it happen all at once, a lightbulb
flickering into a light
that brings my shadows
into unloveable focus?

when will she leave?
when will she decide she has had enough?
when will the novelty of loving me wear off
when will i empty
all of my drawers?

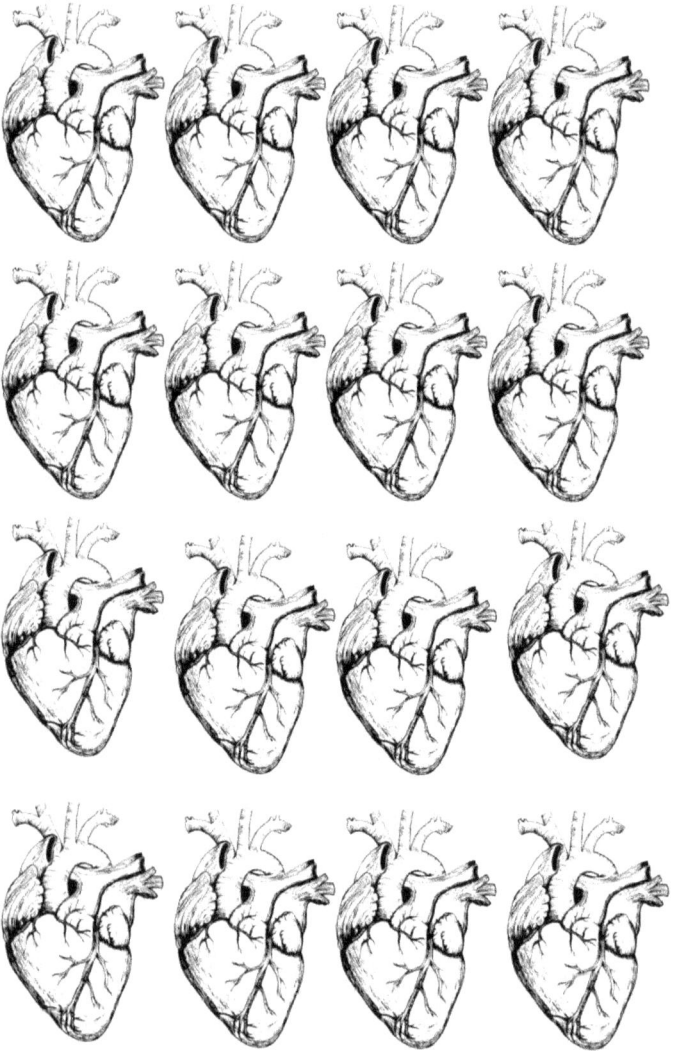

BACKHAND - (32)

flinch
you haven't touched me
how is it that
he can
still
reach me?

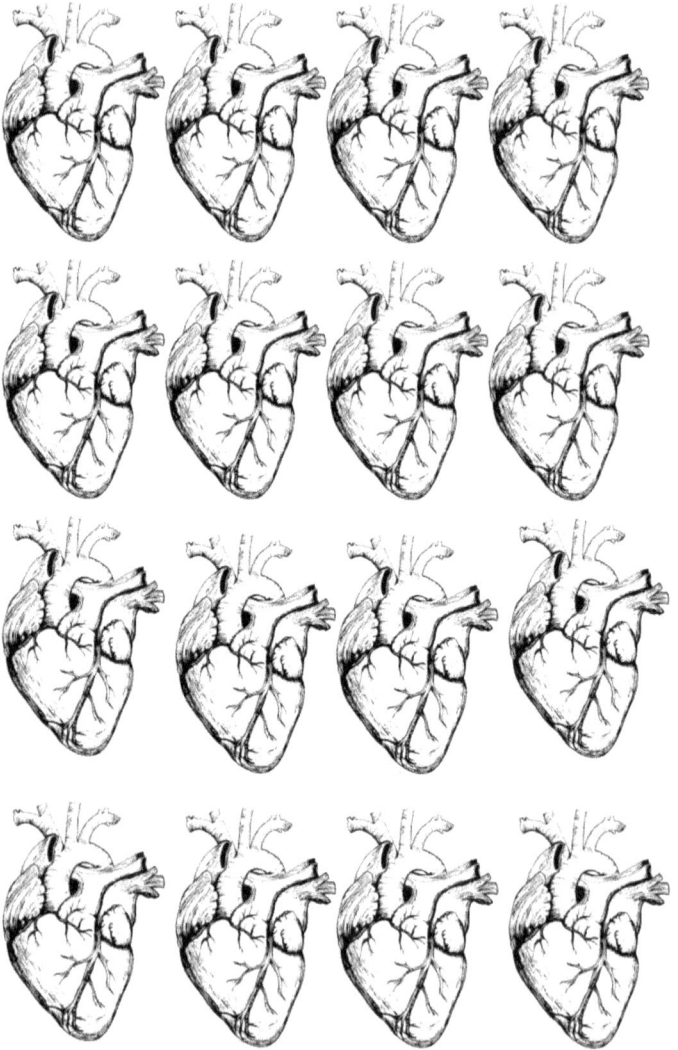

KEBRIT - (33)

i put out the fires
where is all this smoke coming from
i put out the fires
why is there ash in your mouth
i put out all the fires
he is dead and gone
a ghost lives in my closet
i can hear the rattle of his bones

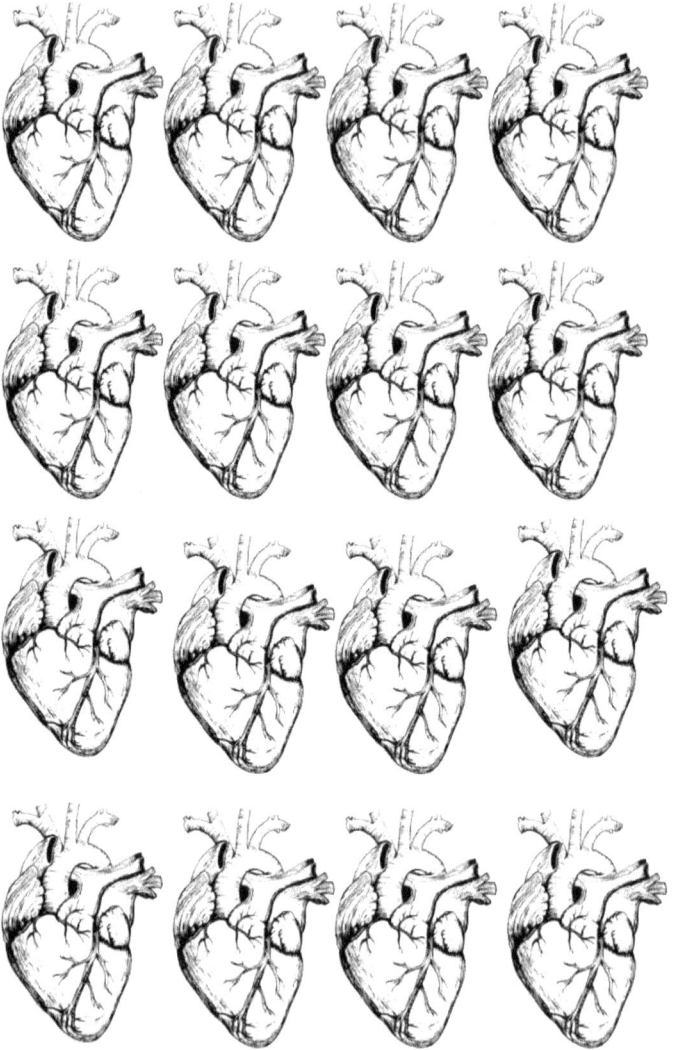

WE ARE THE BEGINNING - (33)

i am happy even when comparison
poises itself as
the thief of joy
i scramble looking for connections
a thread that i'm eager and fearful
to pull
what might unravel
if i find you like the same cologne
if you have the same smile
when you laugh at my jokes
i am afraid i love people into hating me
and that someday you might become
someone i need to forget
that my brokenness will break us
and you will come to hate me
with shards on your lips

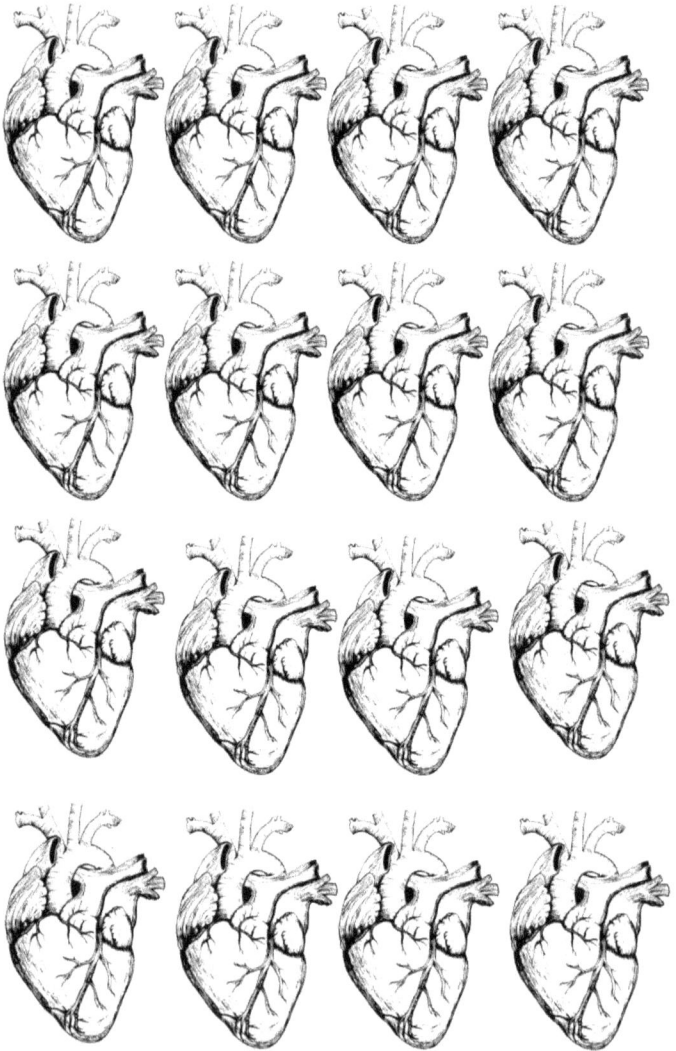

I KNOW WHERE LOVE LIVES - (34)

my mother never met him
but she has met you
she knows your distain for sour things
which rules out most of our cultural foods
she also knows how hard you try
to learn and try something new
because you are not him
and you love me
almost as much as i love you

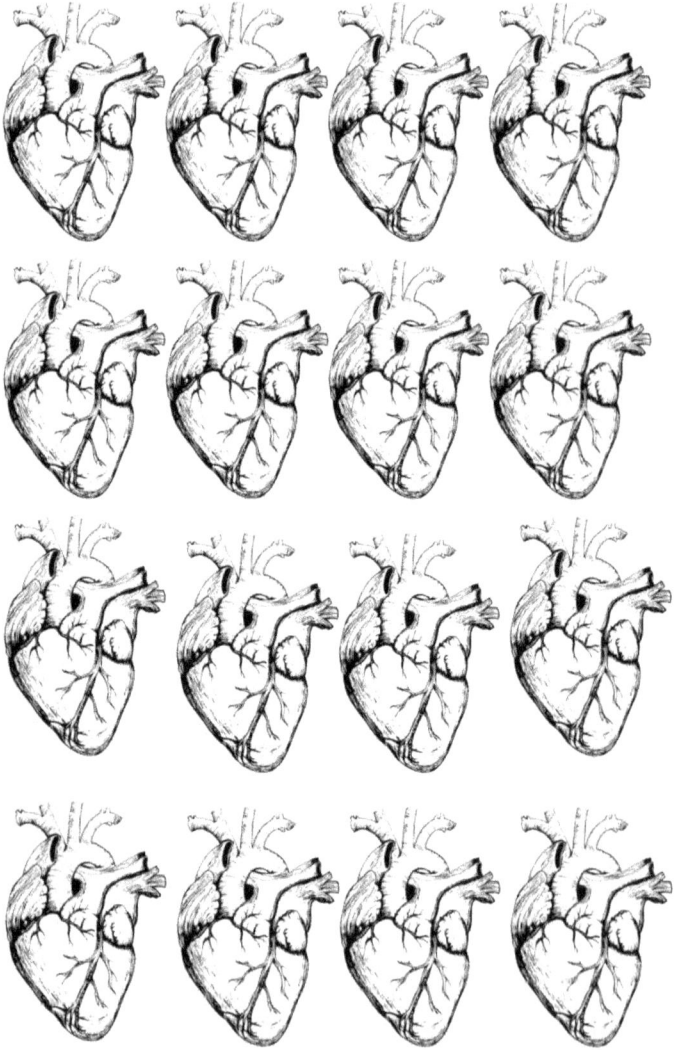

EXORCISMS ON MAIN STREET - (35)

i banish the thought
that i am unworthy
to be loved softly like this
as if the wars could deter me
from the sweet embrace of your kiss.

i deserve to be loved by you
in this soft, calm way
without storms or water walled up
crashing onto us so we dissolve in a wave.

you are every river
love leads to
and i will drink you in forever
my heart is parched for only you.

don't leave
i won't beg
because i can survive alone
i just like who i am with you.

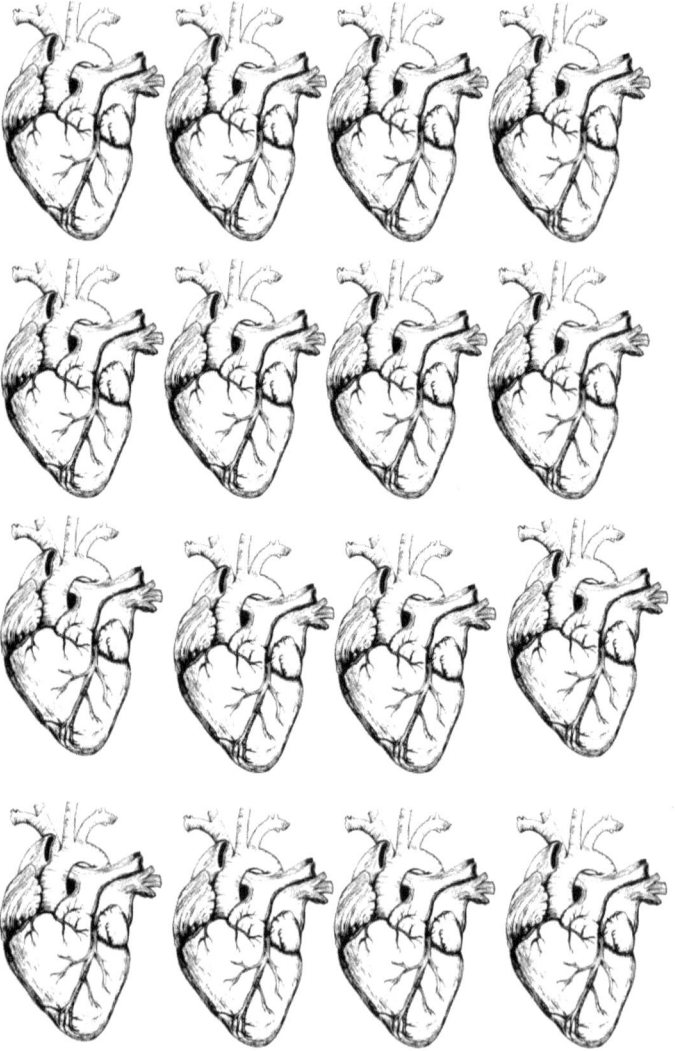

A PETTY POLTERGEIST - (36)

you are more than
the ghosts that haunt you
your story is a reckoning:
how to build and restore
what you did not break
how to exorcise the pain
and let in something new

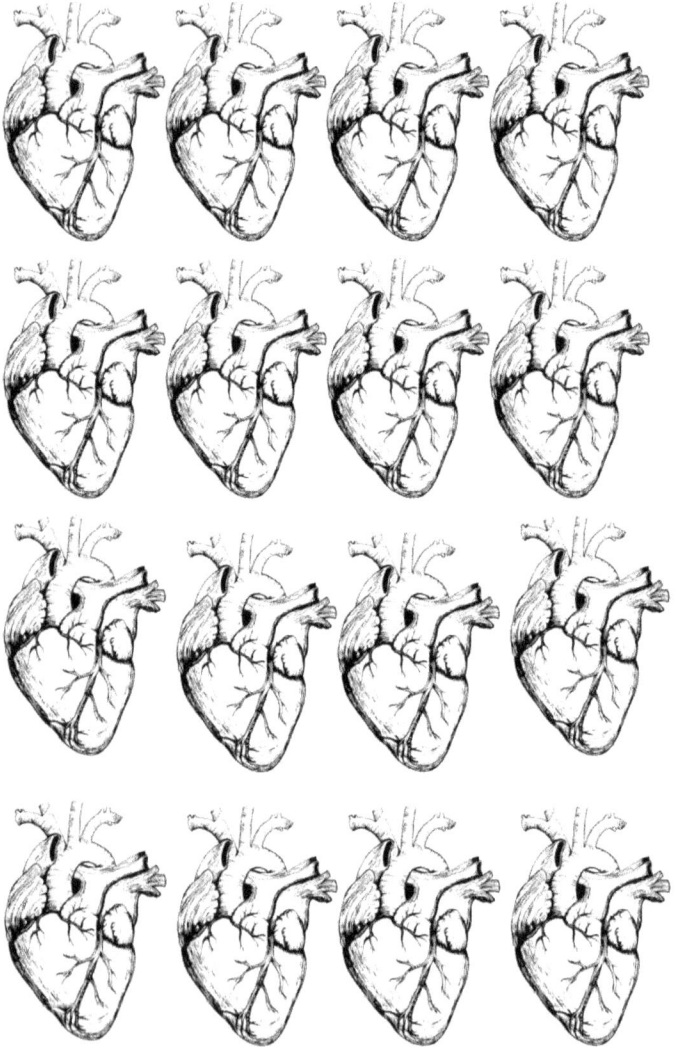

GOODBYE, DJINN - (37)

the world did not end when he left
but it did begin again
when i met *her*

the version of myself that
doesn't live or die by
who loves me
approvals i claw for
kneading a gentle resting place
validation
whispers
bruised wrists
i am all the love
i need to sink my teeth into

dear reader,

finding this book in this moment was not by chance. it came to you as all things do —with divine, unknowable purpose. it is to remind you of your strength. to commemorate your battles. there is no wound that can be wielded against you once you accept the bleeding and choose to heal.

i hope you found what you needed here.

love,

pardis

Intimate partner violence has been labeled an epidemic in Canada. If you or someone you know needs help, please see some of the resources below. From a secure browser, you may also visit **www.victimconnect.org/resources/national-hotlines/**

Canadian Numbers and Resources

Sheltersafe.ca: Provides information and a **clickable map** to help connect women and their children across Canada with the nearest shelter for safety and support.

Ontario

1. Assaulted Women's Helpline: 1-866-863-0511 (toll-free, 24/7, multilingual service available)

on your Bell, Rogers, Fido or Telus mobile phone: #7233

2. Fem'aide 24/7 Support Line: 1-877-336-2433 (French only)

3. Ontario 24/7 Community and Social Services Helpline: 211

4. Talk4Healing 24/7 Helpline for Indigenous Women: 1-855-554-4325

5. Victim 24/7 Support Line: 1-888-579-2888

6. **iHEAL app**: A free, private and secure app to help Canadian women who have experienced abuse from a current or past partner to find personalized ways to stay safe and be well.

British Columbia

1. VictimLinkBC: 1-800-563-0808 (toll-free, 24/7, multilingual service available)

2. Battered Women's Support Services Crisis Line: 1-855-687-1868

3. BC 24/7 Community and Social Services Helpline: 211

4. Youth Against Violence Line: 1-800-680-4264

5. WAVAW Rape Crisis Centre's Crisis and Information Line: 1-877-392-7583

Alberta

1. Family Violence Information Line: 1-780-310-1818 (toll-free, 24/7, multilingual service available)

2. Alberta Abuse Helpline: 1-855-443-5722

3. Alberta 24/7 Community and Social Services Helpline: 211

4. Alberta's One Line for Sexual Violence: 1-866-403-8000

5. Distress Line: 780-482-4357

Quebec

1. SOS violence conjugale 24/7: 1-800-363-9010 (bilingual service available)

2. Crime Victims Assistance Centres: 1-866-532-2822

3. Helpline for Victims of Sexual Assault: 1-888-933-9007

4. Quebec Community and Social Services Helpline: 211

5. Women Aware Support Line: 1-866-489-1110

6. Youth Protection Services: 1-800-567-6810

Manitoba

1. Domestic Abuse Crisis Line: 1-877-977-0007 (toll-free, 24/7)

2. A & O: Support Services for Older Adults Intake: 1-888-333-3121

3. Klinic Crisis Line: 1-888-322-3019

4. Klinic Sexual Assault Crisis Line: 1-888-292-7565

5. Support for Crime Victims and Witnesses: 1-866-484-2846

Saskatchewan

1. Mobile Crisis 24/7 Helpline: 306-757-0127

2. Saskatchewan 24/7 Community and Social Services Helpline: 211

3. Saskatchewan 24/7 Response and Crisis Lines

4. Prince Albert and area: 306-764-1011

5. Saskatoon and area: 306-933-6200

6. Regina and area: 306-757-0127

Nova Scotia

1. Neighbours, Friends and Families (Abuse and Violence Support Line): 1-855-225-0220 (toll-free, 24/7)

2. Adult Protection Services: 1-800-225-7225

3. Avalon 24/7 Sexual Assault Helpline: 902-421-1188

4. Eskasoni 24/7 Crisis Line: 1-855-379-2099

5. Nova Scotia 24/7 Community and Social Services Helpline: 211

New Brunswick

1. Chimo Helpline: 1-800-667-5005 (toll-free, 24/7)

2. After-Hours Emergency Social Services: 1-800-442-9799

3. Beauséjour Family Crisis Resource Centre

    o 506-533-9100 (daytime crisis line)

    o 506-312-1542 (evening crisis line)

4. Crossroads for Women 24/7 Crisis Line: 1-844-853-0811

5. Sexual Violence New Brunswick 24/7 Sexual Assault Support Line: 506-454-0437

Newfoundland and Labrador

NL Sexual Assault Crisis and Prevention Centre 24/7 Support and Information Line 1-800-726-2743

Northwest Territories

1. Native Women's Association of the NWT 24/7 Crisis Line: 1-866-459-1114

2. NWT Help Line: 1-800-661-0844 (toll-free, 24/7)

3. YWCA NWT 24/7 Crisis Line: 1-866-223-7775

Nunavut

1. Kamatsiaqut Nunavut Helpline: 1-800-265-3333 (toll-free, 24/7)

2. Emergency Measures 24/7 Line: 1-800-693-1666

3. Qimavvik Shelter 24/7 Crisis Line: 867-979-4500

Prince Edward Island

1. Island Help Line: 1-800-218-2885 (toll-free, 24/7)

2. Adult Protection Services: 902-368-4790

3. Chief Mary Bernard Memorial Women's Shelter 24/7 Crisis Line: 1-855-297-2332

4. PEI Family Violence Prevention Services 24/7 Crisis and Support Line: 1-800-240-989

www.ingramcontent.com/pod-product-compliance
Lightning Source LLC
Chambersburg PA
CBHW060039040426
42331CB00032B/1549